Zen Shaolin Karate

禅少林道

Zen Shaolin Karate

The Complete Practice, Philosophy, and History

Nathan Johnson

CHARLES E. TUTTLE COMPANY

Rutland, Vermont & Tokyo, Japan

Disclaimer

Please note that the publisher of this instructional book is NOT RESPON-
SIBLE in any manner whatsoever for any injury that may result from practicing the techniques and/or following the instructions given within. Since
the physical activities described herein may be too strenuous in nature for
some readers to engage in safely, *it is essential that a physician be consulted
prior to training.*

Published by the Charles E. Tuttle Company, Inc.
of Rutland, Vermont, and Tokyo, Japan
with editorial offices at
1-2-6 Suido, Bunkyo-ku, Tokyo 112

LCC Card No. 93-60525
ISBN 0-8048-1918-1

First edition, 1994

Printed in Japan

This book is dedicated to all those
who can realize the value of karate beyond fighting
by digging deep enough in the mud
of their own limitations
to reveal the gem that is to be found there

Victory breeds hatred
The defeated live in pain
The peaceful live happily
Giving up victory and defeat
—*Dhammapada 201*

Contents

Chapter Three
Saam Chin 64

Acknowledgments

My thanks go to my parents, James and Barbara Johnson; my wife, Eleanor May-Johnson; Elaine and Terry May; and *sangha* members (past and present) of Chithurst Buddhist Monastery.

My thanks also go to Mr. Dave Franks, co-discoverer of the Nai Fuan Chin applications; Mr. Mike Stobart; Sensei Steve Rowe of Shi Kon Karate Kai; and the Three Unknown Men.

Many thanks to Pat Stockley and Amber Matthews for the photography, and Shao Cheen Laine for her artwork.

I am grateful to Mr. Patrick McCarthy, Director of the International Ryukyu Karate Research Society, who gave me permission to use the photos of Gichin Funakoshi and Choki Motobu, and the British Museum for the use of the photo of Chinese bronze statues.

Finally, I would like to thank Meik Skoss for his editorial guidance, and the staff of the Charles E. Tuttle Company.

Foreword

by Steve Rowe

Chief Instructor, Shi Kon Karate Kai
Contributing Editor, *Traditional Karate* magazine

This book represents a milestone in the martial arts; it contains all the necessary ingredients to become a classic. Nathan Johnson has poured his heart and soul and a significant part of his training life into this work. He has 'burned the midnight oil' with his research into historical martial art texts and worn out the bodies and patience of his training partners in his quest to produce a generation of well-balanced karate-ka (karate practitioners).

The concepts contained within these pages are well researched and practical. They make sense of many of the kata (preset solo martial art forms) movements practiced by modern karate-ka for no other reason—until now—than that they were 'traditional' or with applications that have obviously been made up after the original ones were lost. The whole of this text is imbued with the wisdom of the ancient masters and Nathan manages to communicate these precepts in such a way that they reach out from the pages and touch the heart as well as the mind. That in itself makes this book a classic.

His research has broken all the barriers between the different nationalities and their prejudiced ways of presenting their own martial arts. In our workshops we have had people from many different martial backgrounds 'pushing hands' together under Nathan's guidance, exploring their similarities instead of their differences. It really does herald a new era where, instead of jealously guarding their 'secrets' from successive generations and allowing their art to disintegrate, modern instructors are sharing and learning from each other to improve their systems and then documenting them so they are not lost to those wishing to follow the way in the future.

Read this book with an open heart and an open mind and just let the philosophy wash over you, because the secret of all martial art technique lies in the weight of the practitioner's heart, not his hands or feet.

Introduction

Karate has become a household word in many countries of the world. It is a far cry indeed from the days when it was practiced as an obscure Okinawan village art. As a word, karate simply means empty hand (*kara* = empty, *te* = hand). Karate originated in China where the empty-hand arts grew as an extension of the ancient teachings of the *Ch'an* (Zen) monks of the Shaolin Temple. In fact, the true teachings reflect this ancient wisdom in a practical way. If a system is stripped of its essential philosophy, it becomes nothing more than a gross collection of methods for brutalizing our fellow human beings. Fear is a poor substitute for respect.

The great classics in any art form serve as a source of inspiration to the succeeding generations. They are the bedrock upon which future developments depend. True karate teachings can be said to be contained in the original solo forms, or kata, which preserve the classical art. Of the utmost importance in the preservation of these classical kata is the soul of each form, its practical function.

This book is about classical karate. However, far from being dry or safe, it is controversial. It breaks totally new ground, not through innovation but through the restoration of the neglected practical applications of two of karate's oldest and most profound kata. These are woven together to form a concise and highly practical system that remains true to the wisdom of the Shaolin Temple and that is enjoyable to learn and practice.

This book reveals the Chinese origins of karate and how to unite and apply all the techniques shown. Most of these kata applications have never been published in English. You are invited to try them for yourself, and if you like them, to make them your own.

Chapter One of this book deals with the Shaolin Way and the history and background of karate. Chapter Two deals with basic techniques and exercises. Chapter Three deals with the Saam Chin kata and Saam Chin boxing (boxing is given to mean punching, striking, kicking, and deflecting). Chapter Four deals with the Nai Fuan Chin kata (note that this is in fact three kata in one) and Nai Fuan Chin grappling (joint locks, restraints, and throws). Chapter Five deals with the ultimate combination of the techniques in Chapters Two to Four through the medium of pushing hands, which forms the bridge or link between kata and application.

The karate in this book can be categorized as Zen Shaolin Karate, which means the empty-hand (way) of Shaolin meditation. It is not a style, however, but a living principle. Its major characteristics are strict adherence to Zen principles, and a refusal to use self-generated power or to initiate an attack. In fact, Zen Shaolin avoids direct confrontation (in which the strongest win), instead seeking the watercourse way (the line of least resistance), flowing with the lines of force, and turning an opponent's force back on him. In so doing, the need to become aggressive is removed.

Using genuine applications, you can also overcome the limitations of strength because you will not be using it! You will learn how to absorb your opponent's force, borrow, and then give it back, the whole process being done instantly by contact reflex while the mind is dispassionately fixed in the meditational state known as *samadhi*. If you find your body is flowing with the force of an attack, not resisting or blocking, but rerouting it, and if you find calmness amidst physical action, then you will have discovered the watercourse way for yourself. Your own understanding will lead to your own true karate-do.

Gassho

Nathan J. Johnson

Kai San, Zen Shaolin Karate Renmei
The University of Southampton

Chapter One

Philosophy and History

To begin, I will describe the history of karate, from its origins at the Shaolin Temple through to its development in Okinawa and eventual transplantation in Japan. In this chapter, I will also outline the philosophy and theory of the art, which are inseparable from the its physical aspects.

The Shaolin Way

The Shaolin Temple (Shorin-ji in Japanese) stood in a misty, mountainous region in China's Honan Province. The name means "Temple of the Young Trees" and was so-called because of the small trees that surrounded it. Prior to its destruction in 1644 or 1645, an observer could have watched the temple's monks practicing martial arts forms in the early morning light and again at twilight. It was here in this temple that many of the empty-hand fighting arts evolved greatly as they became an extension of Buddhist meditation. The monks began a system of combat training in which they learned how to counter an attack without resistance, conscious thought, or aggression. This was the forerunner of what was later to be called Eighteen Monk Boxing. These techniques were compiled into forms, some of which became popularly known by the Japanese term kata. We are sometimes encouraged to imagine that the empty-hand arts somehow grew from these exercises independent of the rest of Buddhist practice, but if we are to gain any insight into the true value of the empty-hand arts, then a basic understanding of the essential philosophy is required.

Zen is the Japanese translation of the Chinese word *Ch'an,* which in turn is the Chinese translation of the Indian word *dhyana,* meaning meditation. According to tradition, its founder and first patriarch, Bodhidharma (Daruma in Japanese), left India and crossed into China, eventually taking up residence in the Shaolin Temple (*circa* A.D. 528).

The monks practiced seated meditation, living in the moment, and the direct experience of reality. It is said that Bodhidharma often pointed to wild animals or natural beauty to directly convey a teaching without using words. How many of us have not felt a tugging, somewhere deep within, when exposed to an ink drawing of a Zen landscape (or any other art form bearing the hallmark of Zen simplicity)? For many centuries, teachers have used these direct methods to transmit the concepts of Zen, which are always better experienced than discussed. The direct method also

reduces the need to engage in endless and often counter-productive intellectual discussion.

What Is Zen (as Related to Karate-do)?

Many people who hear the words Zen meditation have a safe intellectual category for them or assume that they know what meditation is, without even trying it! One common misconception about meditation is that it is sitting down and thinking of nothing. This is completely wrong.

Meditation teaches absolutely focused concentration on one point. The meditator will swiftly bring the mind back to that point if it wanders. This provides strength and the ability to completely concentrate, born not from struggling, but from letting go, relaxing, and not following casual thoughts. Often an untrained mind lacks discipline in concentration and may retreat into a daydream at an inopportune moment. In fact, the untrained mind will often do anything in order to escape the moment. During our schooldays, many of us were reprimanded for lapses in concentration. A standard instruction was "Pay attention!" This is all very well, but for some of us, we might just as well have been told to jump 30 feet into the air. No one ever told us *how* to pay attention. For some it comes more readily than others, but many of us need to be taught to do it effectively.

To practice Zen is to pay attention. Meditation teaches us to become masters of our thoughts, and not their slaves or victims. During the meditation process, no attempt is made to reject or suppress thoughts. One simply tries to disengage oneself from them, so as not to get caught up in them. Thoughts are simply identified and let go by returning the mind to the point of concentration without punishing oneself.

This is a primary practice of Zen, however, this method still remains subjective, personal, and solitary. The alternative method of Moving Zen, in this case training between pairs, was devised from the brilliant clarity of Zen practice. This practice consisted of 'rolling hands' and 'pushing hands' drills, which are unique forms of contact training. Using these methods, a training partner's movements could be read or felt with the body through arm contact. With the arms acting in the same way as an insect's feelers, the type, direction, and magnitude of a force (be it a push, punch, grab, etc.) could be determined and dealt with instantly and without thinking. In this way, practitioners would be engaged in a kind of two-way meditation.

The Shaolin monks were not intending to fight as such, though their methods were undoubtedly effective. However, their intentions could easily have been misconstrued by lay members of the community, non-Buddhists, or anyone with a wish to fight. To all intents and purposes, this kind of moving meditation between pairs of trainees was never meant to be a way of overcoming anything other than the aspirants' own delusions. Bias, fear, and aggression were left behind as one learned to break free from the trap of self-limitation. By transcending both virtue and vice, one was put in harmony with the great Void.

From the Zen point of view, when aggression and fear arise in the mind and we act upon them, we are being controlled by our emotions and the urge to fight and dominate others will replace the watercourse way. Although Shaolin training began with the programming of prearranged drills, during the more advanced stages of study free practice was used. Experienced monks and nuns must have presented an impressive, even formidable appearance as they neutralized and countered all manner of attacks during their martial arts practice.

In the early Ch'ing dynasty, the empty-hand arts became divorced from their original, underlying philosophy.

Shaolin Temple guests, rebels, and refugees from the Manchu armies tried to adapt Shaolin empty-hand arts to mundane utility in warfare. Tales about fighting monks and Buddhist warriors are highly suspicious. A warrior monk, referring to a fighter ordained as a Buddhist cleric, is a contradiction in terms and a violation of office. Any monk bearing arms would be immediately disgracing his vows of ordination and violating the Buddha's noble precepts. Most stories of warrior monks are found in popular Chinese fiction, dealing with the late Ming through the Ch'ing dynasty (1644–1911). They are, in general, tales about marauding rebels dressed as monks. This helps to explain why the Manchus found it necessary to burn the Shaolin Temple, a supposed religious place, to the ground. From a military point of view, the confusion of the times left them with no option.

Later still, corrupted versions of the Shaolin fighting arts filtered down to the common people of China through organizations with political purposes, the forerunners of the triads. By that time, they were inexorably linked with fighting and the formal ties with Zen were all but severed as popular ignorance threw away the wheat and kept the chaff. Street peddler kung fu (a Cantonese name for theatrical empty-hand fighting) became popular as crowds were drawn by its display of elaborate kung fu forms and mock combat. These forms even found their way into Chinese opera and touring theatrical groups. Even so, some of the true forms were passed down. A good guide to these original forms is the previously mentioned Zen hallmark of *simplicity*. The central philosophy behind these forms is still Zen.

During the last three hundred years, other theoretical elements have been attached to the practice of the fighting arts, but these do not constitute the roots of the practice, and are merely a reflection of the practitioners themselves. Any art, be it music, painting, dancing, etc., may reflect the culture in which it is practiced. In the West, where competition and achievement are important elements of that culture, it is not surprising that the fighting arts are practiced competitively. Similarly, in Japan, where the warrior spirit was for centuries central to Japanese culture, we find that modern writers have associated karate with bushido, or the way of the warrior.

It is not my intention to denounce either bushido or martial arts competition, but I do believe that we must recognize these as cultural influences that have been attached to the Shaolin empty-hand arts. They are not central philosophies that govern its practice.

Okinawan Karate History

Our search for the origin of modern karate-do takes us from China to Okinawa, the main island of a group known collectively as the Ryukyu Islands. These islands, which were a tributary state and trading partner of China, are situated some four hundred miles east of the Chinese mainland and three hundred miles south of the Japanese islands. The Okinawans had frequent contact with the Chinese mainland, and Fukien Province in particular. It is through this contact that the Okinawans learned Chinese empty-hand forms.

The three states that originally made up Okinawa were unified by King Sho Hashi in 1492. Soon after taking power, he banned the possession of all weapons. In 1609, Okinawa was invaded by the Satsuma clan from Kagoshima, which continued the weapons ban. After the initial Satsuma occupation, peace was soon restored and the garrison left behind was only a nominal one. Some popular legends claim that karate was devised in order to combat the Japanese warriors, either bare-handed or with primitive weapons, but the Satsuma samurai were well-equipped, well-trained, formidable soldiers, and it is highly unlikely that unarmed techniques could prevail against these armed warriors. These popular legends also fail to account for the Chinese names of kata and the Buddhist names of some of the postures that can still be found in Okinawan karate.

It is much more likely that the Okinawans initially learned the Shaolin empty-hand arts from traveling monks, traders, seafarers, and those fleeing in the wake of the Manchu conquest of China. By blending and synthesizing many styles and techniques, and adding their own ideas, the Okinawans came up with several unique empty-hand schools. These were characterized by three major recorded approaches: Shuri-te, Tomari-te, and Naha-te, each giving rise to their own distinctive *ryu,* a martial tradition.

Bronze statue of Chinese wrestlers
from the Chou dynasty (1122–221 B.C.)

Zen Shaolin Karate

Karate, as such, was practiced in Okinawa but its kata are primarily derived from Chinese forms and its methodology originally included *t'ui shou* (pushing hands). The various schools of karate each used different selections of kata as the basis for their style. It is not surprising, therefore, that the same forms appear in different styles. There was inevitably some crossover. Some kata have been modified and others have been invented fairly recently, but most were practiced for many years in and around the villages of Shuri, Naha, and Tomari. These three villages are all within a few miles of each other and collectively influenced the development of Okinawan karate.

These three basic approaches to karate were taken to the Japanese mainland during the 1920s. As the worldwide popularity of karate has come about since its transmission to Japan, we will now turn our attention to its development there.

Japanese Karate History

The development of karate in Japan is a fairly recent phenomenon. One of the most prominent and enthusiastic early teachers of karate in Japan was an Okinawan named Gichin Funakoshi. Often called the father of modern karate, Funakoshi began to introduce karate to Japan during 1922. He was not the first Okinawan to do so. It is recorded that Choki Motobu had moved from Okinawa to Osaka in 1921, and was engaged in teaching karate in that area. However, it is quite clear that Gichin Funakoshi exerted the most influence on the development of karate. He transformed Okinawan karate into a Japanese art by infusing it with concepts taken from Japanese budo (literally, martial ways). Funakoshi further changed the names of the kata for reasons of his own and he reorganized karate terms in conformity with kendo, Japanese fencing.

Gichin Funakoshi

The provincial art of Okinawan karate soon began to undergo a radical revamping. This took place through the teaching of karate in Japanese colleges and universities, and the tireless efforts of leading enthusiasts of the day. At that time, systematic experimentation with various forms of sparring began. Karate (as taught by Gichin Funakoshi) tended to be centered around the group performance of kata, with little training in application, so his students innovated and spearheaded a new approach that included much more prearranged and free sparring. This took karate in a new and popular direction and led to the formation of large, well-organized groups such as the Japan Karate Association.

28

Choki Motobu

These groups have pioneered the modern tournament systems, borrowing heavily from the methods used in kendo competitions, and karate has in recent years been promoted as a sport. If, however, we wish to understand and fully utilize the benefits of the ancient kata and the intentions of their creators, then a return to the original source is required. This does not amount to an actual rejection of modern ideas, but if you use a wrench to hammer in screws, do not blame the tool or its manufacturer if you hit your hand or produce poor work. The same applies to the proper study of karate, its underlying purposes, and training methods.

The Ancient Kata

A kata is a prearranged sequence of movements that can be practiced alone. Kata have been handed down to us by the masters and teachers of the past as messages in movement. While karate has proliferated into an uncountable number of styles, the ancient kata remain. Unfortunately, changes to the ancient kata have appeared, particularly since the transmission of karate to Japan and the rest of the world. No matter how subtle a change may be, over the years it will make a great deal of difference, just as a one degree error in a compass or map reading will take you farther away from your intended destination the more you travel.

Because the earliest recorded teachers of karate in the eighteenth century are so remote and shrouded in legend, and because they have left nothing in writing, the only directions we can follow are the ancient kata themselves. It is easy to see the need for a precise knowledge of the intentions of a kata's creator (*i.e.,* what it is for). If the function has been understood and the skill assimilated, there is no need to change the kata. If we accept that the ancient forms were created by those who knew what they were doing, then they are indeed the bedrock upon which the empty-hand arts rest. If modern interpretations do not match them or make any sense, we should look again to the kata, rather than willfully alter them to suit our purposes! One of the major reasons for the changes to some kata that appear in modern karate systems is the lack of understanding of the original meaning and function of the individual movements and general patterns contained in each form.

Function Dictated Form

True kata were developed by observing and recording how the human body could successfully respond to direct forces: rolling with, rerouting, and turning that force back on the sender. Continuous contact is an important element, and this accounts for the lack of Western-style ducking and weaving. This hands-on aspect of both the Saam Chin and Nai Fuan Chin kata means that an opponent's arms or legs are continuously monitored by contact, then trapped or neutralized. Neither of these kata make any sense at all as a choreographed fight against multiple opponents and should not be considered as such.

Although these kata are performed solo, the information that they contain gives rise to practical formulae that dictate, as simply as possible, the science of unarmed combat. Attempts to apply any kata without prior understanding of its essence (if it is a genuine kata it will have one), produce highly individualized applications that bear little resemblance to the original purpose of the form. These individualistic interpretations are so unlimited in scope that a situation arises in which you cannot see the wood for the trees, and collecting more and more kata will not help. Unless you can penetrate to the essence, the kata will remain a mysterious set of movements that are very difficult to apply in a practical way.

The real skill lies not in the static or mechanical repetition of a kata, or in acquiring a familiarity with an endless number of forms, but in the practitioner's ability to apply the kata with a training partner, and to improvise spontaneously on its given formula or theme.

The kata is the systems manual for all aspects of karate, including fighting, and should not be considered a separate practice. If students spar in ways that do not accurately utilize or even resemble the range of methods illustrated in the kata of their school, then the shortcut sparring methods will prevail, the kata will become superfluous, and the proven way will be lost.

Chapter Two

Basics

In this chapter I will introduce the physical aspects of the art beginning with a brief description of some exercises that may be useful for warming up. Following that I will describe the stances, basic strikes, and kicks that need to be perfected before one can begin to study the Saam Chin kata and its application. I will finish with a description of the rolling techniques that are so vital for the safe practice the Nai Fuan Chin applications in Chapter Four.

Warming Up

If you believe, as was traditionally the case, that the purpose of karate is either exercise or practice of the art's theories, then the kata become the warm-up for those activities. Zen Shaolin karate does not make any use of the squat-thrusts, jumping jacks, body toughening, or many of the other preparatory movements often found in karate classes. Instead, it uses the traditional kata to prepare the body for the specific exercise in which it will be involved, the application of the kata.

The Zen Shaolin karate warm-up method involves practicing the Saam Chin kata and then the more mobile Nai Fuan Chin kata. While performing these kata, no use is made of *kime* (focus) because stiffness or jerky tension is extremely detrimental to the correct practice of Zen Shaolin karate. Also, it should be noted that Saam Chin and Nai Fuan Chin contain no ballistic movements, so one should not throw full-power punches or kicks into thin air as they can hyperextend the elbow or knee.

The need to warm up is apparent, with the most common reasons being getting the body going, "heating" the body in order to avoid injury, and stretching so as to be able to punch, strike, and kick. Convinced that we must prepare the body for a grueling challenge, or pseudo-combat, it is still easy to become confused about how we are to warm up most effectively. Warm-ups need to achieve three things: first, to raise the pulse rate; second, to provide movements for mobility; and third, to stretch the body. The degree to which this takes place is, of course, dictated by the type of activity being pursued (*i.e.*, a table tennis player will warm up in a different way to a sprinter). It is doubtful whether the ancient founders of karate practiced the full splits or the whole host of gymnastic and athletic exercises seen in the modern karate warm-up. The general feeling of modern practitioners is that the ancient masters were not as educated or as scientific as we are. This book postulates the reverse, that the old masters' methods contain a true science based on sound body mechanics, symmetry, and safe, economical movement. They may not have been able to explain it in modern terms, but they could do it!

The aims and objectives have changed in modern karate. I do not wish to degrade or in any way devalue flexibility. I simply wish to encourage a more reasonable approach, making long-term and short-term safety equally important for karate students.

Far from being old-fashioned, traditional karate kata (with their high stances) parallel very accurately the findings of modern sports science, which state:

- There is a fine line between flexibility and joint stability. Some gymnasts can suffer dislocation injuries as a result of the excessive flexibility of their tendons and ligaments.
- The best way to warm up is to approximate as closely as possible the exercise in which you will be involved. Zen Shaolin karate's main activity is the application of kata through pushing hands practice. By starting slowly with small movements, the range and scale of movements can be gradually increased, but without ever going beyond the natural range of movement. Hyperextension (attempting to or actually extending a joint beyond its natural range of movement) is to be avoided.
- Recent research has determined that the safest maximum angle of flexion for a weight-bearing leg is 60 degrees. This angle is adhered to in the original 'high' karate stances. To make the stances unnecessarily deep during kata means, of course, that you will need a warm-up in order to practice what should be the

karate warm-up. After that, you will also need a warm-down. This sort of karate training will become a more athletic pursuit, with the natural outcome that the more robust will excel. The result of this approach is a type of karate that will look strong, and some people will benefit from it. However, it will be despite the way they practice and not because of it.

Perhaps it is time that karate got away from the 1950s rugby-type warm-up and started looking forward by looking backward to the original tradition! Modern sports scientists have found that many of the established modern karate warm-up exercises are dangerous, so be careful. The maxim for Zen Shaolin karate is "natural is best."

Auxiliary Warm-up Exercises

If auxiliary exercises are required, the following warm-ups may be used. The emphasis is on gently stretching the body. These exercises can, of course, be added to. As with all exercises, never force anything or hold the breath, unless specifically instructed to do so.

Exercise One—Stretching the Neck: Stand relaxed, feet shoulder-width apart, and bend the neck forward and backward, and to the left and right, holding each position for a count of five. Repeat several times.

Exercise Two—Circling and Stretching the Arms: Stretch and swing the arms 15 to 20 times. Begin by stretching the arms forward in front of your hips, palms down. Raise and cross your arms in front of your chest, palms inward. Stretch your arms overhead, palms up, then lower them to your shoulders with your arms extended and palms out to the sides. Finally, lower your arms to waist level, palms forward, hands beside your hips.

Exercise Three—Swinging the Arms and Twisting the Hips: Twist your body around your hips and swing the arms around your body. Relax the whole body and allow the hands to touch your back as you swing. Repeat 15 to 20 times.

Exercise Four—Circling the Hips: Gently circle the hips in both directions, clockwise and counterclockwise. Repeat this movement 10 to 15 times. Avoid making abrupt, jerky movements.

Exercise Five—Bending at the Waist and Stretching the Hamstring Muscles: Stand with your arms folded in front of your chest and your feet one-and-a-half shoulder widths apart. Breathe out as you slowly bend forward with your hips, touching your elbows to your legs, going as low as you comfortably can. Repeat this exercise ten times. Then, breathing normally, keep your legs as straight as possible as you try to grasp the ankle of one leg with both hands. Bring your head as close to your knee as you comfortably can. Bend and stretch first to the left leg, then to the right. Repeat this exercise 20 times.

Stances

Exponents of Zen Shaolin karate do not fix themselves in postures that show a willingness to fight, just as one does not shout when holding a handful of aces in a poker game. From a defensive point of view, the height and depth of a stance are determined by the strength, type, and direction of an opponent's force. In effect, an attack will cause one to flow into a particular posture. With the exception of the use of the Saam Chin stance during fixed pushing hands practice, Zen Shaolin karate stances are not fixed positions. They should be flowing and constantly changing according to the degree of force, the intended target of an attack, and the condition of the terrain. Stances serve as a base from which to

1   1¹ *(another view)*

deliver force to a training partner, or to absorb and return a force.

All stances should be learned and practiced on both sides. With the exceptions of the neutral stance and the offensive stance, the hand positions shown have no real importance while the stances are being learned.

Neutral Stance

Stand symmetrically with the feet one shoulder width apart and the weight evenly distributed. Keeping the back straight, relax the body, and let the shoulders drop. Close the mouth and breathe through the nose (Figs. 1, 1¹).

This stance is used when there is no contact with an opponent and the distance is such that a step would need to be taken before an attack could take place. There is no guard or position to adopt at this point. Preparation should simply be confined to *zanshin,* which is an alert, relaxed state of awareness, or "remaining mind."

2   2¹   *(another view)*

Offensive Stance

Stand with one foot forward, as if you had moved one foot directly forward from the neutral stance by one-and-a-half shoulder widths while rotating the hips approximately 45 degrees. Keep the back straight and bend the front leg so that the knee is directly above the ball of the foot. Seventy percent of the weight is supported by the front leg, and 30 percent by the rear leg. Turn the front foot slightly in, so it is pointing toward the center. The rear leg can be slightly bent. Each fist is clenched and is positioned on or just wide of the midline, which is a vertical line that goes down the center of the front of the face and body. The front fist is held at shoulder height, such that the back of the fist is vertical and the arm is extended forward (but not completely straight). The rear fist is held slightly lower and close to the chest. Both elbows are down and tucked in (Figs. 2, 2¹).

This stance is used primarily to deliver offensive attacks, and as such is used only to help one's training partner develop his defensive skills.

3

3¹   *(another view)*

Saam Chin Stance

Stand with one foot forward, as if you had moved one foot directly forward by the length of one of your feet from the neutral stance, without rotating the hips at all. Keeping the back straight and your weight evenly distributed, bend both knees slightly inward and turn each foot 45 degrees toward the center. Push the hips forward and grip the ground with your toes (Figs. 3, 3¹).

This stance is used only with contact generally, and in fixed pushing hands specifically.

4   4¹   *(another view)*

Cat Stance

From the Saam Chin stance, keeping the back straight, bend the rear leg deeply so that it supports 90 percent of the weight. Simultaneously bend the front leg and straighten the ankle so that the heel has no contact with the ground, and rotate the hips 45 degrees so that they then face straight along the line of the front leg and foot (Figs. 4, 4¹).

This stance, formed by opening the Saam Chin stance, is used only when in contact with an opponent, where its central function is connected with a pivot that evades an attack and unburdens one leg of body weight.

5   5¹   (another view)

Straddle-leg Stance

Stand symmetrically with the feet parallel, one-and-a-half to two shoulder widths apart, the legs bent, and the weight evenly distributed. Keeping the back straight, relax the body and let your shoulders drop. Do not push the hips forward (as in the Saam Chin stance) or let the buttocks jut out (Figs. 5, 5¹).

This is the primary stance of the Nai Fuan Chin kata, and is often referred to as the 'horse-riding' stance. It provides a strong base from which to grapple with and throw an opponent.

6   6¹   *(another view)*

Crossed-leg Stance

Keeping the back straight and both legs bent, cross one leg with the other. With both feet on the ground, and the heel of the rear, lesser weight-bearing leg raised, point each foot either straight forward or back toward the midline (Figs. 6, 6¹).

    This is the secondary stance of the Nai Fuan Chin kata. It is, strictly speaking, not a stance at all, but a transitory position used in sideward movements to follow an opponent, or to turn a corner. It is also used to maintain the proper contact distance with a mobile opponent. One may also move backward and forward by converting this stance into the cat stance. This is a very practical way of testing the ground because the floating foot only rests the ball of the foot down before transferring the weight.

Basic Techniques

Karate ni sente nashi.
(There is no first attack in karate.)

These words, promoted by Gichin Funakoshi and Shoshin Nagamine, among others, are the embodiment of karate.

All authentic kata begin with a defensive movement. This is not a quaint oriental custom. It is a principle of karate that the opponent's own attack should lead to his downfall and should also provide the impetus necessary to accomplish this task. The following techniques are provided as a set of basic striking methods. They should be thought of as methods of providing attacks to which your training partner can respond. Occasionally, some of these techniques can be woven into the Saam Chin applications and thus be used as alternatives to the basic palm-heel strike found in Section Three of the kata.

These techniques are not meant to be used offensively. Unfortunately in modern karate it is all too common to see people attack for the sake of attacking. In this case, karate practice degenerates into a mere confrontation where two people stand off and try to batter each other from an inappropriate distance. There are no direct blocking techniques in Zen Shaolin karate. Defensive maneuvers, consisting of deflections and trapping, are covered in Section Three of the Saam Chin Application.

Zen Shaolin karate does not concern itself much with the development of self-generated power, for reliance upon it (*i.e.,* power developed from one's own speed, torque, hip twist, etc.) carries with it all the natural limitations of size, strength, fitness, gender, age, and aggression levels.

The common trend in karate of merely equipping practitioners with a collection of blocking and striking techniques that rely upon the amount of power that the individual can produce is reversed in Zen Shaolin karate, where

7

the real skill is in harmonizing or blending with an oncoming attack and redirecting its force back to the attacker. None of the Zen Shaolin basic techniques are studied with a view to seeing how much force one can generate. If you stress self-generated power, it will always be your limitation. Despite this, it is necessary to learn and practice good, clean, accurate basic attacking methods. The basic attacking techniques in Zen Shaolin karate are structured to give freedom and variety while maintaining a systematic, methodical framework. Blows are categorized and recorded according to their point of origin with regard to an imaginary line that runs vertically down the center of the human body (Fig. 7). This line, usually called the midline, should not be considered a line of vulnerable spots on the body.

8

8^1 *(another view)*

Hand Techniques

Lead-hand Straight Punch: From a left offensive stance, thrust the lead fist forward while fully straightening the arm. Rotate the lead fist clockwise until the back of the hand is horizontal. Keep the rear fist close to the chest. Allow the shoulders to rotate slightly clockwise into the technique (Figs. 8, 8^1).

9   9¹ *(another view)*

Rear-hand Straight Punch: From a left offensive stance, punch by simultaneously retracting the lead fist to a position close to the chest and rotating the hips counterclockwise at least 45 degrees thereby causing the rear fist to be thrown forward and the arm fully straightened. The rear fist rotates counterclockwise until the back of the hand is horizontal. Allow the hip rotation to cause the rear heel to lift and the rear knee and foot to turn inward (Figs. 9, 9¹).

Lead-hand Back-fist Strike: From a left offensive stance, rotate the hips clockwise 45 degrees by pivoting on the balls of both feet, reversing the weight distribution between the

10   10¹ *(another view)*

11   11¹ *(another view)*

legs, and position the lead fist over the rear shoulder. Then throw the lead fist horizontally with a whiplike action, allowing the arm to straighten. Keep the back of the lead fist vertical throughout the movement, and the rear fist close to the chest. Allow the hip rotation to cause the front heel to lift and the front knee and foot to turn inward (Figs. 10–11¹).

12 12¹ (another view)

13 13¹ (another view)

Rear-hand Back-fist Strike: From a left offensive stance, rotate the hips counterclockwise 45 degrees and position the rear fist over the lead shoulder. Then retract the lead fist to a position close to the chest and throw the rear fist horizontally with a whiplike action, allowing the arm to straighten. Keep the back of the rear fist vertical throughout the movement. Allow the hip rotation to cause the rear heel to lift and the rear knee and foot to turn inward (Figs. 12–13¹).

14   14¹ *(another view)*

15   15¹ *(another view)*

Lead-hand Hook Punch: From a left offensive stance, reposition and open the rear fist to form a vertical open palm at shoulder height. Pivot on the balls of both feet, rotating the hips clockwise 45 degrees by pivoting on the balls of both feet, reversing the weight distribution between the legs. Rotate the lead arm clockwise until the back of the fist is horizontal. Swing the elbow, and to a lesser extent the fist, well outside the edge of the body and back toward the center. Allow the hip rotation to cause the front heel to lift and the front knee and foot to turn inward (Figs. 14–15¹).

16   16¹ *(another view)*

17   17¹ *(another view)*

Rear-hand Hook Punch: From a left offensive stance, reposition and open the lead fist to form a vertical open palm at shoulder height, close to the chest, while rotating the hips counterclockwise 45 degrees. Then rotate the rear arm counterclockwise until the back of the fist is horizontal. Swing the rear elbow, and to a lesser extent the fist, well outside the edge of the body and back toward the center. Allow the hip rotation to cause the rear heel to lift and the rear knee and foot to turn inward (Figs. 16–17¹).

18   18¹ *(another view)*

Vertical Elbow Strike: From a left offensive stance, retract the lead fist to a position close to the chest, while rotating the hips counterclockwise at least 45 degrees. Then rotate the rear shoulder upward so that the rear fist (the back of which becomes vertical) moves to the side of head, and the elbow swings upward. Allow the hip rotation to cause the rear heel to lift and the rear knee and foot to turn inward (Figs. 18, 18¹).

19   19¹ *(another view)*

Horizontal Elbow Strike: From a left offensive stance, retract the lead fist to a position close to the chest, while rotating the hips counterclockwise 45 degrees. Rotate the rear shoulder so that the rear fist remains close to the chest, and the elbow swings outward. Allow the hip rotation to cause the rear heel to lift and the rear knee and foot to turn inward (Figs. 19, 19¹).

20   20¹ *(another view)*

21   21¹ *(another view)*

Palm-down Knife-hand Strike: From a left offensive stance, open each fist into a knife-hand, while rotating the hips counterclockwise 45 degrees and positioning the rear hand over the lead shoulder, palm toward the ear, fingers pointing backward. Then retract the lead hand to a position close to the chest. Thrust the rear hand forward, across the center of the body, almost fully straightening the arm, and rotate the rear hand counterclockwise so that the palm is facing down. Allow the hip rotation to cause the rear heel to lift and the rear knee and foot to turn inward (Figs. 20–21¹).

22   22[1]   *(another view)*

Palm-up Knife-hand Strike: From a left offensive stance, open each fist into a knife-hand, and position the rear hand over the rear shoulder, with the back of the hand toward the ear, fingers pointing forward. Retract the lead hand to a position close to the chest, and rotate the hips counterclockwise at least 45 degrees, allowing the rear hand to be thrown forward and the arm to almost fully straighten. Rotate the rear hand clockwise so that the palm is facing up. Allow the hip rotation to cause the rear heel to lift and the rear knee and foot to turn inward (Figs. 22–23[1]).

23   23¹ *(another view)*

Leg Techniques

Zen Shaolin does not decry the use of kicking techniques. However, it does not condone excessive reliance upon them or their overuse. When both feet are on the ground, we have balance and mobility. In using kicking techniques (however fast we may be) we are making the largest possible commitment with our largest limb, and thus are sacrificing our stability. Traditional kata contain few kicks. Those that can be found are invariably aimed at low targets so that speed is increased and risk is reduced. Kicks are best employed as counters (*i.e.*, countering a foot sweep or unbalancing attempt).

The maxim for Zen Shaolin leg techniques is that they should require no stretching or preparation. One should be able to perform them at any time.

24   24¹ *(another view)*

Front Kick: From an offensive stance, in one smooth flow-ing movement, lift the rear leg (with the knee and ankle deeply bent) to a raised position directly in front of you, just wide of the midline. Thrust both hips forward, allowing the kicking leg to straighten and the foot to be thrown forward. As you kick, point with the ball of the foot by simultaneously fully straightening the ankle and pulling the toes back. Reverse the positions of the lead and rear hands as the leg is raised. Keep the hips at the same height throughout the movement (Figs. 24–26¹).

25

25¹ *(another view)*

26

26¹ *(another view)*

27   27¹   (another view)

Foot Sweep: From an offensive stance, lift the lead leg (with the knee and ankle well bent and the foot arched) to a raised position in front of the supporting leg. Keep the hips at the same height throughout the movement (Figs. 27, 27¹). Use the inside of the foot to hook your opponent's knee or ankle.

28   28¹   *(another view)*

29   29¹   *(another view)*

Low Side Kick: From an offensive stance, lift the lead leg (with the knee and ankle well bent) to a raised position in front of you. Straighten the lead leg fully, thrusting the foot out diagonally, away from the supporting leg and downward. As you kick, form a sword-edge foot by simultaneously bending the ankle fully, arching the foot, and pulling the big toe back. Keep the hips at the same height throughout the movement (Figs. 28–29¹).

30

31

32

Rolling

Many of the applications of the Nai Fuan Chin kata (refer to Chapter Four) emphasize breaking the opponent's balance. A training partner who resists the technique or does not know how to roll will risk injury if he does not tumble smoothly when being thrown. In order to make the practice of Zen Shaolin karate safe and enjoyable, it is vital to be able to roll. The basic method requires that you establish a reasonable relationship with the ground. Once this has been established through the devoted practice of these rolls, you will be able to practice Zen Shaolin karate's throwing techniques without fear of being injured.

33 34

Forward Roll

Begin by kneeling on one knee, and extend your open left hand (Fig. 30). Keep the chin tucked in and make the body round as you slowly let your body drop and roll forward (Figs. 31–33). Continue forward until you are back in the kneeling position (Fig. 34). Do not rush the technique and do not slam the ground. Gradually increase the speed until you can safely roll without undue thought or effort. When you feel ready, try rolling from a standing position. By training in this gradual manner, it is not essential to have mats below you when you roll.

35 36

37

Backward Roll

As before, begin from the kneeling position (Fig. 35). As you allow yourself to drop and fall backward, keep your chin tucked in and make your body round. Roll across your shoulder blades until your legs go above your head (Figs. 36, 37). Allow the momentum to carry you back to your starting position (Figs. 38, 39). As before, gradually increase the speed until you feel comfortable with the technique.

Zen Shaolin Karate

38

39

Chapter Three

Saam Chin

Saam Chin, which means "Three Conflicts," is the original pronunciation of the more common Japanese name Sanchin. This kata is an excellent example of the brilliance of Shaolin Temple boxing. In terms of depth of meaning, practicality, and simplicity, it is unsurpassed. Unfortunately, in more recent times, there has been a tendency to associate elaborate or flowery forms with the Shaolin tradition and to confine Saam Chin to the so-called Okinawan or Japanese traditions. It is not my intention to open up a partisan dispute but simply to record that the Saam Chin kata originated with the Shaolin tradition as it was continued in Fukien Province in China, where it remains simultaneously the primary and the most advanced boxing form for many Fukien-based systems.

Chojun Miyagi (1888–1953), the founder of Goju-ryu karate, claimed that, "If one practices Sanchin continuously, there is no need to learn anything else. Sanchin is everything." Although Miyagi taught other kata, he was merely following the instruction of his teacher Kanryo Higaonna, who had traveled to China to learn Chinese boxing. The idea was to 'dig a small hole, but go very deep.' While we are quoting the master teachers, it is important to note that it was Gichin Funakoshi who said that, "In ancient times, great experts would not know more than five kata." This is borne out to some extent by the syllabi of other systems, such as Wing Chun, which has only three boxing forms, and t'ai-chi ch'uan, which has only one form as a base.

The name Saam Chin refers to the conflict said to exist between the mind, the body, and the spirit. This conflict is dealt with in three stages:

- *mushin* (nonanalytical thinking in urgent situations; a state of spontaneous response in combat);
- *zanshin* (remaining mind or awareness; automatic awareness);
- *samadhi* (total absorption).

Samadhi

When *mushin* and *zanshin* are combined, a state of *samadhi* ensues. It can be said that *samadhi* is the spirit, in the mind-body-spirit trilogy. By curbing excessive or distorted responses based on emotion (self-consciousness, lack of confidence, outright fear, etc.), interference from the analytical mind is reduced, if not removed. The body, meanwhile, freed from emotional and intellectual constraints, can get on with the job at hand.

Much has been written with regard to spirit. When we remove it from the smoke screen of mysticism that usually surrounds it, we see that spirit is actually the power of a person completely harmonized in mind and body who, in the midst of an activity, manifests complete involvement or absorption and focus of attention on the task at hand.

When *samadhi* appears, there is no longer distinction between subject and object, inside and outside, enemy and

self. Indeed, the idea of self disappears, along with the whole host of worries and problems that assail our waking hours. This complete state of being is not confined to the empty-hand arts, for some sports and participatory art forms can also act as vehicles for the unfolding of focused attention. At advanced levels, this ability can permeate even the most mundane of tasks and is referred to in Buddhist traditions as mindfulness—a mind full of what one is doing, not mindlessness.

As beneficial as this is or may sound, the problem in applying it is consistency. Some golf rounds are better than others. Some practice sessions are great, while others are not very good. These apparent discrepancies hinge on our ability to concentrate and fully commit ourselves.

Achieving Samadhi through the Saam Chin Kata

Attaining a state of *samadhi* is not left to chance during Saam Chin practice. All you have to do is practice the kata! You will, of course, have to pay strict attention to the breathing method used throughout the form. This method of breathing is known in Indian as *pranayama*, which means to restrain the breath, energy, or spirit. It is the key to attaining *samadhi*.

In Saam Chin breathing, the total number of breaths per minute is lowered but the oxygen intake per breath is tripled (without making you lightheaded). This produces a state of calm, focused concentration in which the brain waves change from a beta to an alpha frequency. There is a direct connection between the breath and the physiology of paying attention. Good oxygenation of the brain, attained by keeping a straight back and breathing from the belly and not from the chest, is essential when concentrating in this manner. Breathing correctly and practicing the sequence of the solo kata will lead one to levels of such profound concentration that it becomes possible to rise above superficial thoughts and emotions and enter the mental state known as *samadhi*.

Saam Chin Breathing

To practice Saam Chin breathing safely and effectively, several factors must be considered carefully:

- If you have a medical problem (or are badly out of shape), consult a medical doctor before attempting to practice this breathing method.
- Breathe deeply but lightly, and never force the breath or breathe noisily.
- The basic format is to breathe in with the pulling motions and out with the pushing motions.
- Ensure that the belly swells (so that you appear to be potbellied) as you breathe in.
- After breathing in, ensure that the lower abdomen is firm. There should be no direct muscular tension in any other part of the body except perhaps the grip of the feet on the ground.
- When you exhale, slowly breathe out, contracting or pulling in the abdomen as you do so.
- Ensure that a little breath is still left in the lungs at the end of the out breath. At times you will contract your lower abdominal muscles to hold this remaining breath.
- Do not struggle with the breath. If you become dizzy or lightheaded, stop practicing and try to even out your breathing. If, after considerable practice, you still have trouble with the method, you could add a very short in-out breath at the end of every out breath.

Above all else, remember that as you perform this kata, you should feel a profound sense of well-being and relaxed, quiet concentration.

1   2

Saam Chin Theory

The following are descriptions of the important techniques, postures, and concepts that you will encounter when performing the Saam Chin kata. A thorough familiarity with them is a prerequisite to learning the kata itself.

The Saam Chin Stance

In the solo form, the Saam Chin stance is used to acquire and maintain all the body habits necessary for partner practice. The stance promotes physical and mental stability. One should grip the ground with the feet, push the hips forward, and "sit" on the resulting frame. When the proper stance is achieved, the Saam Chin breathing becomes the most effective. When using the stance with a training partner, it can readily be seen how it provides a sound angled base in which the lead foot's toes point inward at the circumference of an imaginary circle. The following pictures illustrate this circle, which is the first of the three important circular concepts contained in the Saam Chin kata (Figs. 1, 2). The three circular concepts will be discussed below in the section on the impassable ring.

3   4

Whenever you shift from one Saam Chin stance to the next during kata practice, feel the ground with your feet. Do not step mechanically. Read the terrain with the stepping foot (Figs. 3, 4).

The Unbendable Arm

The opening out of the two arms after assuming the lowered crossed-hands posture resembles the unfurling of a crane's wings. This movement helps eradicate the dominance of one side of the body over the other, thus developing your ambidexterity. The arms should be resilient and have a natural elastic tension rather than a heavy muscular contraction. This is often referred to as the unbendable arm.

70   Zen Shaolin Karate

5

To experience the unbendable arm for yourself, hold the arms as shown (Fig. 5). Imagine an outpouring of energy (known in Japanese as *ki*, and in Chinese as *ch'i)* from your energy center (known in Japanese as the *hara* or *tanden,* and in Chinese as the *t'an-tien)*, which is located about one to three inches below the navel. Feel this energy spreading along your arms like water through a hose. Do not consciously tighten either the biceps or triceps, just keep the angle of the arms constant. Ask your assistant to then attempt to bend your arms. You will be able to prevent this by extending and projecting your energy.

There is nothing mystical at work here for although this experiment can seem quite impressive it is really only a practical demonstration of the natural resilience of a positively charged human limb or a body freed from the self-defeating overuse of antagonistic muscle groups (*i.e.,* the biceps working against the triceps, etc.). In fact, the whole kata should be practiced with a magnificent feeling of positive life force filling the body. When practiced this way, the kata creates a pleasant feeling of well-being.

Coordination of Hand and Arm Movements

The sequence of movements after the unbendable arm need not be considered as blocks and strikes. In fact, with open-handed movements, this is not a very practical idea. The founders of Goju-ryu karate changed the open-handed movements contained in this section to closed fists, in conformity with Okinawan ideas. These movements teach one the ability to move the arms independently of each other and the rest of the body. The importance of developing and maintaining this ability will be explained in Section Three of the Saam Chin Formula. Also note that the arm and wrist circling that concludes Section One can be employed to reverse positions or free a gripped wrist.

The Impassable Ring

The impassable ring is one of three defensive circles introduced in the Saam Chin kata. It is the middle circle and the area within your arms when performing this technique could be called the pushing hands buffer zone because it is a key position in that practice. This position is used to keep your opponent and his attacks a minimum distance from your body. This will provide a noncollapsible barrier around which you can redirect all attacks. Within this area the body will turn, pivot, or step in order to neutralize an attack. This second imaginary circle is also depicted by the arms as they are turned by the waist during pushing hands practice (Fig. 6). As you will see in Chapter Five, by switching hand techniques, neutralizing the attacker's force by a movement at the waist, or a combination of the two, any attack can be redirected.

As was mentioned earlier, the first (or lower) circle is the area between your feet while in the Saam Chin stance. The lower circle provides stability so that you can effectively counter all of your opponent's attacks without losing your

6

balance even while moving from stance to stance. The third (or upper) circle is the cycle of catching, trapping, detaining, and counterattacking movements that is introduced in Section Three through the circular parry.

The impassable ring sequence in Section Two of the Saam Chin kata restores the arms to equality and provides a set of arm movements that are the reverse of those in the first section. In Section One, the wrists are out and the elbows are in, while the forearms are in a vertical position. In Section Two, the wrists are in and the elbows are out, while the forearms are extended in a horizontal position.

Coordination in Saam Chin

The movements in Section Three of the kata combine the body habits acquired in the first two sections. In summary, the sequence goes like this: in Section One, each hand moves independently of the other and the rest of the body; in Section Two, both hands are moved together and perform the same role; in Section Three, both hands move simultaneously but each one performs a separate and independent role.

7   8

The passing, trapping, and returning of an attack requires the use of both hands at the same time. Although the hands perform separate roles, they are functionally integrated. This is quite distinct from the more modern karate methods of using only one limb at a time, or of striking without trapping or controlling an opponent's limbs.

As was mentioned before, this circular parry depicts the third (or upper) circle. Although the lower and middle circles are both horizontal, the upper circle involves both horizontal and vertical circular movements. It should be performed smoothly and without undue tension.

Merging with an Attack

To withdraw from or to knock aside an attacking force is to waste its potential energy. Moreover, it does not help one's overall position or help to control or neutralize an opponent. Section Three of the Saam Chin kata provides a method whereby we can merge with and utilize this oncoming force. The method has three distinct phases: in phase one, the hand goes out to intercept and merge with an oncoming attack (Figs. 7–9); in phase two, the force is drawn in with one hand (in harmony with the direction of that force) and swiftly rerouted by the other trapping hand (Figs. 10, 11); in phase

74   Zen Shaolin Karate

9

10

11

12　　　　　　　　　　　　　13

three, the same hand that originally performed the interception returns the force with the palm-heel strike (Figs. 12, 13). These three phases need to be harmonized into one smooth flowing circular action that an opponent or training partner could interrupt at any point. If you are operating a 'dead' block or mindless sequence, you will never be able to apply the formula in a satisfactory way. You must be aware at all times of what your opponent is doing in response to your techniques. It is of vital importance to develop sensitivity to force in the arms, which act like insects' antennae, ever ready to detect an attack. Note that the capture of the opponent's limb also allows you to lead him off balance and into a situation in which he must discontinue his attack (Figs. 14, 15).

It is not realistic to assume that every punch or push can be countered, so you need to be prepared to continue the cyclic meeting and trapping of hands until you have achieved sensible control of one of the attacks. By far the best medium in which to practice and develop this skill is pushing hands, where the constant contact will allow you

76　　　　　　　　　　　　　　　　　Zen Shaolin Karate

14   15

to better monitor and more quickly meet an oncoming attack. This method is a basic guideline, not a dogmatic absolute. It can be improvised upon, although it does contain the most direct method for dealing with a variety of attacks.

The Palm-heel Strike

The palm-heel strike is delivered by smoothly extending the vertical palm forward from a position that is close to the chest and just wide of the midline. Keep the elbow down and tucked in. Do not fully extend the arm, for the striking point, the fleshy base of the palm, should make contact with the target while the elbow is still bent.

Unlike the fist, the palm requires no conditioning and is more flexible in its uses. It can control, pin, trap, grasp, and push more readily than the fist. The palm causes less superficial damage (cuts, abrasions, etc.) than the fist but the force is fully absorbed by the target. The effect of transferring energy through a skillfully applied palm-heel strike can be imagined by likening the fist to a hardwood club, and the palm-heel to a thick rubber tube filled with lead!

Chapter Three: Saam Chin   77

16   17   18

Saam Chin Solo Sequence:
Section One

Assume the attention posture: stand with your heels together and your spine and arms straight, with your hands open at your sides with the palms inward (Fig. 16).

 Do the *gassho:* bring the hands together in front of the chest with the fingers pointing upward and hold the position for a second or two (Fig. 17). Perform the *gassho,* which is a Buddist salutation, at the start and end of all kata and when training with a partner. Return to the attention posture (refer to Fig. 16).

19   20

While inhaling, assume the raised crossed-hands posture: keep the elbows down, and bring the hands together
in front of the chest. The back of the right hand is touching
the left palm, and the elbows are bent approximately 90
degrees (Fig. 18). Begin to exhale and assume the lowered
crossed-hands posture: pivot the hands at the point of contact, and move the elbows outward. As you straighten the
arms, move the elbows back and inward. The palms remain
toward the chest as you fully straighten the arms (Fig. 19).
Continue to exhale and lower the hips by bending the knees
directly forward. Move the right foot forward and outward
in a clockwise horizontal quarter-circle, and assume the
Saam Chin stance (Fig. 20). Completing the exhalation,
form two unbendable arms: move the still-touching hands
slightly forward and turn them in vertical arcs about the

21   22

elbows to shoulder height. The palms face inward, and the upper arms do not move. The angle of the elbows is greater than 90 degrees. Both arms are now at the same height and in the same position (Figs. 21–24).

While inhaling, withdraw the left hand (fingers pointing forward, palm facing upward) to the left side of the body in a horizontal clockwise arc passing just above the right elbow (Figs. 25, 26). Begin exhaling, and move the left hand forward and slightly downward so that the left elbow is straight and at the same height as the other as you turn the

23

24

25

26

27

28

29

82

Zen Shaolin Karate

30

31

palm to face downward (Figs. 27, 28). Finish exhaling, and form a left unbendable arm: move the elbow slightly inward, and the hand in an elbow-centered vertical semicircle. The hand travels inward, upward, and outward so that the palm faces inward. The arms are again at the same height and in the same position (Fig. 29). Holding your breath, move the left foot forward in a counterclockwise semicircle, and assume the Saam Chin stance (Figs. 30, 31).

32   33   34

Perform the three-movement sequence of withdrawing, straightening, and forming the unbendable arm with the right arm, and then step forward with the right foot (Figs. 32–38).

Remaining in this stance, perform the three-movement sequence of withdrawing, straightening, and forming the unbendable arm four more times, first with the left arm then the right (refer to pp. 81–82, then Figs. 39–43, and repeat both sets).

35

36

37

38

39

40

41

86   Zen Shaolin Karate

42

43

44

45

46

47

Zen Shaolin Karate

48   49

Without stepping, and breathing as before, use the left
arm to perform the first two movements of the previous
three-movement sequence, withdrawing and straightening
the arm only (Figs. 44–47). Continue to exhale, while moving the right elbow slightly outward. Rotate the wrists counterclockwise so that the inner wrists face each other, and bend
the wrists back (Fig. 48). Then position both hands in front
of the chest with the palms facing upward so that the elbow
angle is more than 90 degrees, and straighten the wrists. The
arms are again at the same height and in the same position
(Fig. 49). Finish exhaling, keeping the elbow at an angle of

more than 90 degrees, and rotate both arms so that the elbows move outward to chest height and the hands describe small vertical circles (first downward, then outward). Finish with the palms facing downward, and the hands extended further to the sides than the elbows. Although you keep the wrists flexible during the circling movement, straighten them again, and a ring is formed with the circled arms. While holding the breath, hold the position for a moment (Figs. 50, 51). This hand position is known as the impassable ring.

52   53   54

Saam Chin Solo Sequence: Section Two

While inhaling, clench the fists and withdraw both of them, each with a straight wrist, to the side of the body with the palm facing upward (Fig. 52). While exhaling, open the hands, and rotate and partially extend both the arms so that the impassable ring is formed again (Figs. 53, 54). While holding your breath, remain in this position for a moment.

Perform the previous two-movement sequence of withdrawing (clenched fists) and extending (opened hands) both arms three more times, making sure to perform the movement in an even manner (refer to Figs. 52–54).

Saam Chin Solo Sequence: Section Three

While inhaling, move the right foot backward, in a counter-clockwise semicircle into the Saam Chin stance. Perform the circular parry: move the right hand upward and to the right, then across in front of the head to the left, with the fingers pointing upward, in a vertical counterclockwise arc. Simultaneously rotate the wrist counterclockwise horizontally (Figs. 55, 56). The arm moves to the right and backward diagonally across in front of, and close to, the upper chest. Finish in front of, and almost touching, the left shoulder (Fig. 57). Here the right palm is turned so that the fingers point upward. Simultaneously the left hand is moved in a large vertical counterclockwise arc. The left hand first sweeps downward, across in front of the right hip to the right, and then upward and across in front of the head, finishing with the fingers pointing to the side (Figs. 58, 59). The left hand then continues downward and backward, finishing with the palm still facing forward and the fingers now pointing downward. Simultaneously retract the right hand to a position beside the ribs with the fingers pointing upward (Fig. 60). Exhale completely, keeping the palms and fingers vertical

Zen Shaolin Karate

55

56

57

58

59

60

Chapter Three: Saam Chin

61   62   63

with the elbows down and tucked in. Extend both hands forward, but do not fully straighten either arm (Fig. 61). Then, while holding the breath, hold the position for a moment.

Step backward with the left foot, repeat the circular parry with your hands reversed, and extend the hands forward (Figs. 62–67).

94

64   65

66   67

Chapter Three: Saam Chin   **95**

68   69   70

While inhaling, assume the raised crossed-hands posture: move the right foot next to the left foot, and keeping
the elbows down, bring the hands together in front of the
chest with the palms facing inward. The back of the right
hand is touching the left palm, and the elbow angle is
approximately 90 degrees as you fully straighten your legs
(Figs. 68–70). Exhale and assume the lowered crossed-
hands posture (Fig. 71).

71   72

73   74   75

To complete Saam Chin, switch the position of the top hand from left to right and then mirror the previous movements (refer to pp. 79–97) using the right hand to do what the left did previously and vice-versa. Finish in the lowered crossed-hands posture (Figs. 71–75).

76   77

Repeat the *gassho* movement and return to the attention posture (Figs. 76, 77).

Saam Chin Applications

Although defensive skills against single and compound
attacks are best developed through pushing hands practice,
there are a number of practical applications from the Saam
Chin kata. The theories of Saam Chin boxing and examples
of the Saam Chin defenses against specific attacks follow.
In the defensive sequences, the person on the left will be
referred to as **A**, and the person on the right, **B**.

Using the Palm-heel Strike

The Saam Chin kata forms the base of the Zen Shaolin boxing method. In this kata we find no offensive movements at
all, and the only counterattack is a palm-heel strike (which
is sometimes interpreted as a double-palm push). Sole reliance upon this counter might seem to be limiting for in the
world of modern karate, students are encouraged to develop

a huge array of natural weapons, including the fingertips, the knuckles, the edge of the hand, the wrist, the elbow, the knee, and the foot. Yet anyone looking for a logical, systematic, or progressive use of these anatomical weapons will not find it in traditional kata.

Also conspicuous by their absence from these kata are many popular modern techniques. For example, the roundhouse kick occurs in only one traditional kata, Unsu, and even there it is not performed from a standing position.

For the modernist, what is even more perplexing about traditional kata is the apparent lack of realistic combinations of striking techniques, as used by Thai boxers and the like. Some teachers mistakenly claim this is because of the 'one hit, one kill' rule in which one should be able to kill any antagonist with a single blow. The 'one hit, one kill' principle is an old samurai sword fighting concept that was grafted onto the practice of unarmed techniques. If your opponent has good footwork and defensive skills, stopping him with one blow is difficult if not impossible. The reality is that unless you are immobilizing an opponent, breaking his balance, and trapping at least one of his limbs, multiple-strike combinations are also impossible to use except when your training partner delivers a technique and then stays absolutely still! Failure to trap and immobilize an opponent, to control his posture, or to break his balance, results in a confrontational pugilistic-type of karate. This is based not on the aforementioned skills but on the use of ballistic force, speed, aggression, and power.

The traditional kata that originated in China tend to be concerned with harmonizing with and deflecting an opponent's force. They also contain the principles that allow effective covering and trapping of compound attacks, combinations of several strikes. You are now in a position to understand the apparent simplicity of the palm-heel strike in Saam Chin. The most important point about the striking method is not the conditioning of the striking points or the strength of the muscles in the arm, but simply the skill to be able to use it. This skill needs to include the following points:

- You should have control of or be trapping at least one of the opponent's limbs.
- You should be in a superior position, making deflection and counter part of the same circular movement —simultaneous attack and defense—and borrowing force from the opponent's attack.
- You should lead your opponent and keep him off balance so that he cannot use his strength against you.

When the requisite skill has been acquired, the palm-heel strike will take place naturally, as part of a spontaneous but coordinated response. Although one normally aims the strike at the chin, jaw, or nose, with practice, the target becomes self-selecting; one feels the target rather than consciously selecting it. The palm can then be used to press, push, or tip the head back, or to generally upset an opponent's balance. It is said that masters of the Shaolin palm method could defeat an opponent without even hurting him!

The Midline

The Saam Chin Formula provides a key to dealing with an uncountable variety of attacks without treating each one differently and therefore having to assign to it a particular blocking technique. That only works when the attacking method and target are prearranged. According to the Saam Chin method, a strike should be categorized according to its point of origin with regard to an imaginary vertical line that runs down the center of the face and body. No matter which limb an opponent attacks with, you need only consider which side of the midline it comes from. For example, a lead-hand backfist strike is dealt with in the same way as a rear-hand straight punch, because they both originate from the same side of the midline.

78   79

The Significating Hand

When using your right hand to intercept attacks, all attacks that originate from the right side of your midline (your opponent's left side) are met with your right hand and quickly transferred to your left hand. If another attack were to follow, the same right hand would be used to intercept again. Attacks originating from the left side of your midline (your opponent's right side) would also intercepted with your right hand and transferred to your left hand. The intercepting hand is called the significator.

Do not switch your significator or pivot unnecessarily. Still treat attacks coming from the same side of the midline the same way but simply do not change your significator. Having a safe side (working with an unchanging significator) will prevent confusion when you are put under the pressure of combat.

The Chinese called the two sides of the forearm the sky bone and the earth bone. Standing with your hands at your sides, palms inward, the forward-facing side of the forearm is the sky bone, or radius, and the backward-facing side, the earth bone, or ulna (Figs. 78, 79).

80   81

Evasion and Stepping

There are several points you should always keep in mind when evading an opponent's attack using the Saam Chin boxing method:

- Avoid trying to step outside a punch unless you are in the process of deflecting and trapping it. If the attacking arm has a bend in it (as it is when performing a hook punch) you could get caught!

- No guard is needed when a gap exists between you and your opponent. If he is close enough to hit you without stepping, you should already have your arms up and be in 'touch' contact.

- When moving to meet or deflect an attack, move either sideways and forward, or sideways and backwards. If you are intercepting an attack with your right arm, then move to your right.

- Do not expect an opponent to stand still after having delivered one straight punch. You must get used to meeting and deflecting combinations of attacks.

102

82

83

84

Defense Against a Back-fist

A, in a neutral stance, faces B, in an offensive stance (Fig. 80). B chambers a lead-hand back-fist, aimed at A's head (Fig. 81). A evades by stepping to the right, and parries B's attack with his right hand (Fig. 82). A then switches hands and counters with a right palm-heel strike to the head (Figs. 83, 84).

85

86

Defense Against a Lead-hand Straight Punch,
Rear-hand Straight Punch Combination

A, in a neutral stance, faces B, in an offensive stance
(Fig. 85). B aims a lead-hand punch at A's head. A moves
inside the line of B's attack (Fig. 86). A intercepts B's punch

104   Zen Shaolin Karate

87

88

with his right arm, which is now his significator (Fig. 87). **A** transfers the contact with **B**'s offensive left arm (and therefore the force) over to his left arm as he shifts outside **B**'s line of attack (Fig. 88).

89

90

A traps **B**'s extended left hand with his left hand and begins to counter with his right hand (Fig. 89). **B** frees his previously trapped left hand and aims a right punch at **A**'s head (Fig. 90). **A** intercepts **B**'s punch, again with his right arm, or significator (Fig. 91). **A**, having transferred the con-

91

92   93

tact with B's attacking right arm, and therefore the force,
over to his left arm, grasps B's right wrist (Fig. 92). A de-
stroys B's balance by pulling and twisting his restrained right
wrist, and counters with a right palm-heel strike to B's chin
(Fig. 93).

94   95

Defense Against a Front Kick, Rear-hand Straight Punch, Lead-hand Hook Punch Combination

A, in a neutral stance, is pushed by B, in an offensive stance (Fig. 94). B does a half step forward with his rear (right) leg, bringing it level with his front (left) leg (Fig. 95). B raises his left leg as he prepares to attack A with a front kick (Fig. 96). A moves outside the line of B's attack and intercepts B's kick with his right arm, which is now his significator (Fig. 97). A transfers the contact with B's left leg, and the attacker's force, to his left arm (Fig. 98). B places his kicking leg down and aims a rear-hand (right) punch at A's head (Fig. 99).

108

96

97

98

99

100

101

102

A intercepts B's punch, again with his right arm (Fig. 100). A, having transferred the contact with B's attacking right arm over to his left arm, grasps B's right wrist (Fig. 101). B frees his previously trapped right hand and aims a left hook punch at A's head (Fig. 102). A intercepts B's punch, again with his right arm, which is still his significator (Fig. 103). A transfers the contact with B's left arm (and therefore the force) to his left arm and **he** grasps B's left wrist (Figs. 104, 105). A, continuing to restrain B's left wrist, counters with a right palm-heel strike to B's chin (Fig. 106).

103

104

105

106

Chapter Four

Nai Fuan Chin

No forms have remained such an enigma, in terms of credible, practical applications, as the three Nai Fuan Chin kata. Yet, solo performance of the first of them is required to obtain black belt ranking in many major karate organizations worldwide, where these kata are also known as Naihanchi, Naifuanchi, and the well-known Gichin Funakoshi rendition, Tekki, which means "Iron Horseman." Throughout this book, I shall keep to the original Chinese name for these kata: Nai Fuan Chin, which means "Internal Divided Conflict."

The most widespread problem with the Nai Fuan Chin kata is that practitioners of modern karate styles have attempted to represent them as boxing kata. This is an interpretation that continues to dominate to the present time. Attempts to use Nai Fuan Chin movements to block and strike multiple opponents have always lacked serious credibility, yet these applications have been perpetuated for want of anything better! They are not designed for blocking and striking at all. They are in fact a series of restraints, arm and wrist locks, takedowns, and throwing techniques, all performed against a solitary opponent with whom contact is never lost.

The reader will note that I have divided the kata into three sections but have not named the sections Shodan, Nidan, and Sandan. The reason I did this is that in truth Nai Fuan Chin is a single form that has been broken into three parts (no doubt to make it easier to teach). So as not to confuse readers who come from karate systems that divide the kata into three parts, I have retained this division in this text.

The origin of the Nai Fuan Chin kata is obscure but it may have been developed using movements from the T'ang-lang (Praying Mantis) or Ch'in-na (a Chinese grappling system) schools. In Okinawa, they were taught to beginners before the creation of the Pinan, or Heian, kata in 1907.

It is also interesting to note that the Tekki were three of the four kata demonstrated by the founder of modern Japanese karate, Gichin Funakoshi, and Shinken Gima in 1922 at the mecca of Japanese martial arts, the Kodokan. This demonstration created support for karate among several people of power and influence and was thus a turning point in the development of Japanese karate.

Throughout the Nai Fuan Chin kata, there appears to be a preoccupation with escaping from a crossed-arm position that the uninitiated may claim is impractical or contrived. This objection might seem reasonable, given the exact sequence of events that occurs during each symmetrical, two-man application. However, it must be understood that these floor patterns are traditional teaching modules and through practicing these crossed-arm applications, one is able to systematically learn the essential skills of joint manipulation and control, of leading an opponent, and of timing throws to gain maximum effect with minimum effort.

Sometimes crossed-arm situations do arise, and the Nai Fuan Chin responses are very practical, but Nai Fuan Chin practice is not limited to these kinds of circumstances. The techniques can be improvised upon using a single-hand grip, in which it is usually necessary to use the free hand to unbalance the opponent's body in a circular fashion. This skillful but demanding approach can be cut short by using brutality. For instance you could, when grabbed, strike at the throat, eyes, or groin and then perform a throw. To do so, however, would not be in accordance with the wisdom and teachings of Zen or the theory of the watercourse way. In the Nai Fuan Chin kata, there is no need for such crude tactics.

Those obsessed with practical application should heed this warning! Of course the need for instant practicality exists, but it must not impede the development of real skills. We must entrust ourselves to the classical teachings of our predecessors, and must foster the patience and discipline necessary to perfect authentic techniques.

In this book, you will find examples of both one and two-handed Nai Fuan Chin applications. They are in no way complete, serving only as guides and indicators as to what can be done. The rest is up to you. This is a practical workbook, so please work with it.

Finally, as most versions of the Nai Fuan Chin kata have been modified and altered for use as a boxing kata, I have chosen to follow the beautifully accurate kata sequence that Shoshin Nagamine, 9th Dan, *Hanshi*, Shorin-ryu karate-do, demonstrated in the seminal work *The Essence of Okinawan Karate*. I would like to thank him from the bottom of my heart for carefully preserving and recording the solo sequences of Naihanchi (Nai Fuan Chin) Shodan, Nidan, and Sandan in the aforementioned book.

Nai Fuan Chin Grappling

Recording grappling, locking, and throwing techniques in a kata is obviously made difficult by the tremendous number of choices that can be made with regard to the content, order of techniques, the directions for stepping, and so on. The Nai Fuan Chin kata solves these problems by limiting the format to the application of combined grips, operated from a crossed-arm position. Thus, the applications are not self-defense sequences, but a systematic record or catalogue of grip reversals (reversal in the sense that the person being gripped becomes the one doing the gripping) and grappling techniques. Cataloguing grappling techniques in this way prevents the solo form from becoming an esoteric dance, and further provides a classic or traditional teaching. These grappling techniques are developed through the use of the Nai Fuan Chin fist and applied using the Nai Fuan Chin grips. When one has sufficient experience performing the techniques laid down in these traditional two-armed versions, variations and improvisations using one arm, pivots, turns, and steps will begin to suggest themselves.

The Nai Fuan Chin Fist

This unique, apparently obscure method of clenching the fist has sadly fallen into disuse for reasons that will become apparent. The history and use of this fist, however, are worth considerable study.

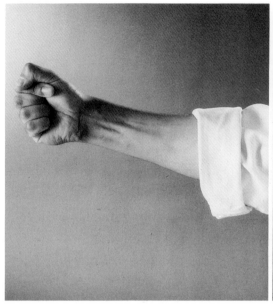
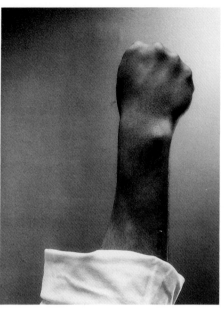

1   2

Clench the fist as shown, emphasizing the grip of the little, ring, and middle fingers. Keep the first joint of the index finger straight and wrap the thumb around it as shown (Fig. 1). The back of the hand should form a straight line with the forearm, and the knuckles should line up with the ulna and radius as shown (Fig. 2).

This strange-looking fist first appeared in print, to my knowledge, in three early books on karate by Gichin Funakoshi: *Ryukyu Kenpo Karate* (1922), *Rentan Goshin Karate Jutsu* (1925), and *Karate-do Kyohan* (1936). In a 1974 English edition of *Karate-do Kyohan,* this fist is illustrated but not explained. Furthermore, the observant reader will be able to see the translator using this very same fist during the photographic sequence of the three Tekki (Nai Fuan Chin) kata. Some exponents of Okinawan Shorin-ryu also still employ this fist.

In modern-day karate, however, this fist has been abandoned. A little investigation with a punching bag or striking post will reveal why: when striking with it you risk dislocation of the first knuckle! So we need to consider why such a fist has been perpetuated in the Nai Fuan Chin kata. The answer is a simple one: it is a method of clenching the fist for gripping.

A solo practice fist that strengthens and trains the little, ring, and middle fingers is indispensable in acquiring good gripping skills. Similar grips can be found in Praying Mantis kung fu and bojutsu (the art of the staff).

In the following pages, we will see the importance of developing three skills and attributes that have been passed on throughout the years and are still emphasized in karate today. They are: a good, strong grip; aligning the back of the fist with the forearm (the strongest position when gripping a wrist); and a strong *hikite* (the pulling back of the hand to the side of the body).

The Nai Fuan Chin Grips

Each section of the Nai Fuan Chin kata starts from a position where the forearms are crossed and each wrist is gripped, and its application begins with two simultaneous grip reversals. The grips acquired by these reversals are as follows: in Section One (*a k a* Tekki Shodan), the combined reverse-hand grip and overhand grip; in Section Two (*a k a* Tekki Nidan), the combined underhand grip and overhand grip; and in Section Three (*a k a* Tekki Sandan), the double underhand grip.

To familiarize yourself with the relative positions of the hands in the noncombination grips, first position one of your hands as in the lowered crossed-hands posture, and have a training partner face you and grab your wrist or lower forearm with his diagonally opposite hand, so that his palm is also facing downward in a regular grip, as though shaking hands.

3

4

The Reverse-hand Grip: From the starting position (Fig. 3), expand the gap between your fingers and thumb, and turn your hand to bring this gap to the outer edge of your partner's wrist. Continue to turn your palm to face upward and position your fingers underneath and your thumb on top of your partner's wrist (Figs. 4–6[1]). Keep the opponent's arm stretched. In a single-hand grip application you could use this grip to lead him in the direction you wish.

118   Zen Shaolin Karate

5

5¹ *(another view)*

6

6¹ *(another view of your right hand's position)*

7

8

9

10

11

The Overhand Grip: From the starting position, bring your hand, with the palm still facing downward, to the outer edge of your partner's wrist. Point your fingers and press forward, in order to weaken the opponent's grip. Widen the gap between your fingers and thumb, and position them, fingers on top of and thumb underneath your partner's wrist (Figs. 7–9). Turn your wrist in a counterclockwise spiraling movement and retract it to the side of your body keeping your forearm horizontal to the ground (Figs. 10, 11).

12

13

13¹ *(another view)*

14

15

The Underhand Grip: From the starting position, turn your palm to face the underside of your partner's wrist. Open the gap between your fingers and thumb and position them, fingers to the outer and thumb to the inner sides of your partner's wrist (Figs. 12–13[1]). Continue to pull his hand forward until you are able to lock his wrist and thus control his movements (Figs. 14, 15).

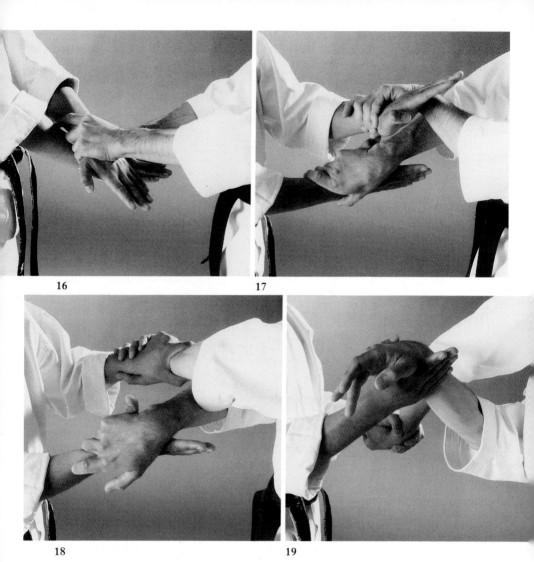

16 17

18 19

The Combined Reverse-hand Grip and Overhand Grip:
If both of your hands are grabbed when they are crossed,
the right hand can perform a reverse-hand grip as the left
hand simultaneously does the overhand grip, crossing up
your partner's arms (Figs. 16–19).

The Combined Underhand Grip and Overhand Grip:
If both of your hands are grabbed when they are crossed,

20

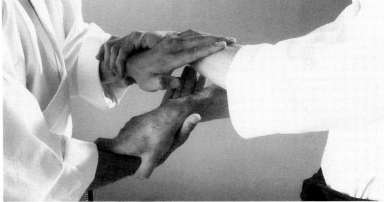

21

22

the gripping movements can be combined in the following manner: the right performs an underhand grip as the left simultaneously does the overhand grip, locking your partner's wrists (Figs. 20–22).

23

24

25

26

The Double Underhand Grip: If both of your hands are grabbed when they are crossed, you defend by performing two underhand grips, locking one of your partner's arms against the other (Figs. 23–26).

The Straddle-leg Stance

The straddle-leg stance is used throughout this kata. When training with a partner, do not stand in a deep stance or you will risk knee injury and groin strain. You will already be close to your limit of flexibility in a deep stance and you will need to stretch further when throwing a partner.

126

27

28

Nai Fuan Chin Section One
Solo Sequence

As with the opening of the Saam Chin kata, begin by assuming the attention posture (Fig. 27).

Do the *gassho*, then return to the attention posture (Fig. 28, then refer to Fig. 27).

29   30   31   32

Assume the raised crossed-hands posture and then the lowered crossed-hands posture (Figs. 29, 30).

Step with the left leg to the right into the crossed-leg stance, and then chamber the rear leg by bending the knee forward and raising it (Figs. 31, 32).

Step with the chambered leg to the right into the straddle-leg stance (Fig. 33). Move the open right hand outward and upward to chest height, keeping the wrist straight and the elbow down and tucked in. Simultaneously clench the left hand into a Nai Fuan Chin fist and pull it to the left side of the body with the palm facing upward (Fig. 34).

33

34

35

Turn the shoulders clockwise 45 degrees and move the left arm upward to chest height and across to the right so that the fist is close to and pointing toward the chest with the palm facing downward. Simultaneously move the open right hand forward and inward so that it is touching the left elbow (Fig. 35).

36   37

38   39

Rotate the shoulders counterclockwise so they are again facing directly forward, and clench the right hand into a Nai Fuan Chin fist. Pull both fists to the right side of the body so that the left hand is above and touching the palm of the right (Fig. 36).

130   Zen Shaolin Karate

40   41   42

Move the left fist outside and away from the left thigh, fully straightening the arm (Fig. 37).

Pull the left fist to the side of the body so it is pointing forward with the palm facing upward. Simultaneously move the right fist in front of the body, palm facing downward, so that the forearm is parallel to the chest but with the fist slightly lower than the elbow (Fig. 38). Step with the right leg to the left into a crossed-leg stance, and then chamber the left leg by bending the left knee forward and raising it (Figs. 39, 40).

Step with the left leg into the straddle-leg stance. Keep the right elbow at a 90-degree angle as you move it downward. Turn the arm in a vertical arc about the elbow until the fist is in front of the right shoulder with the palm facing inward (Fig. 41).

Move the left fist forward and downward (Fig. 42).

43   44

45

Reposition both fists by moving them in counterclockwise semicircles with the palms facing inward (Figs. 43, 44).

    Keeping the left arm in the same position, move the

46   47   48

right fist so it is under and touching the left elbow with the palm facing downward (Fig. 45).

Chamber the left foot by raising it toward the center of the body (Fig. 46). Return to the straddle-leg stance and turn your body counterclockwise 45 degrees. Move the left fist outward and slightly backward, keeping the elbow at a 90-degree angle, and turn it, so that the back of the hand is facing the head (Fig. 47).

Chamber the right foot by raising it toward the center of the body (Fig. 48). Return to the straddle-leg stance, and turn your body clockwise 90 degrees. Move the left fist inward, bringing the elbow back to its position above and

49   50

51

touching the right fist, and turn the hand so that its back is facing forward again (Fig. 49).

In one movement, rotate the shoulders counterclockwise so that they are facing directly forward again. Pull the fists to the right side of the body so that the left one is on top of the upturned palm of the right one (Fig. 50).

Move the fists fully to the left. The right arm does not fully straighten, but the left arm does (Figs. 51, 52).

52

53

54

Assume the lowered crossed-hands posture: move the left foot next to the right foot, open the hands, and lower the arms, with the back of the right hand touching the left palm, while fully straightening the legs (Figs. 53, 54).

To complete Section One of Nai Fuan Chin, mirror the previous movements (refer to pp. 128–135), finishing in the lowered crossed-hands posture.

55

56

57

Nai Fuan Chin Section One
Application

Begin in the Nai Fuan Chin starting position: A and B are
standing facing each other. A's arms are positioned in a similar way to the lowered crossed-hands posture, but are crossed
at the lower forearms. B is firmly grasping both of A's wrists
in a crossed-hand grip (Fig. 55).

136

58   59   60

A extends and firms his wrists and hands, and steps sideways to his right into a crossed-leg stance, moving his left leg across the front of his right. **B** is led in the direction of A's step (Fig. 56).

A raises his right leg, chambering it in order to give momentum to his next movement (Fig. 57).

A steps down and sways his body to his right, leading **B** in the same direction. He then begins to reverse both of **B**'s grips by applying the combined reverse-hand grip and overhand grip (Fig. 58).

A, his arms no longer crossed, establishes a firm grip on each of **B**'s hands or wrists. These grips are retained until the end of Section One. **A** simultaneously extends both his and **B**'s right arm to his right, and turning his and **B**'s left wrist counterclockwise, draws them to the left side of his body. This splits **B** in two different directions (Figs. 59, 60).

61   62   63

B attempts to recover his broken posture by standing erect. A flows with the direction of this movement, and maintaining control of B's right wrist, folds his left wrist and moves it toward his right shoulder. Pushing his left elbow into his right palm, A locks B's wrist (Fig. 61).

A folds B's left wrist and B's already-folded right wrist, and draws them to the right side of his body. This brings B down onto his left knee (Fig. 62).

B attempts to pull himself up onto his right leg. A feels this and leads B by his left wrist in the direction of that movement (Fig. 63).

A simultaneously draws both his and B's left wrist to the left side of his body and presses B's right wrist on the back of B's left elbow joint. This forms a crossed-arm tie, which causes B to roll to his right. A moves sideways with B, in the direction of the roll, and keeps control of B's wrists (Figs. 64–66).

138   Zen Shaolin Karate

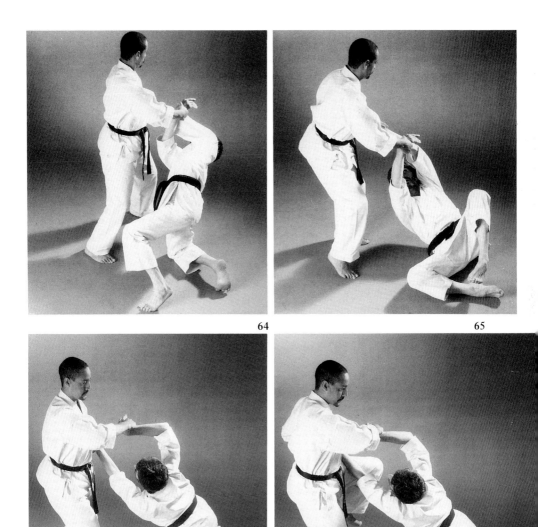

64

65

66

67

*Note: Great care is needed in the application of this tech-
nique. B must be allowed to roll out of the crossed-arm tie at his
own pace or there will be a high risk of injury.*

As **B** is about to come out of his roll, **A** raises his left
leg, chambering it in order to give momentum to his next
movement (Fig. 67).

68

69

70

71

Zen Shaolin Karate

72

73

74

Just as **B** is about to recover his balance, **A** steps down to his left and turns his own and **B**'s right wrist clockwise. This causes **B** to flip over and roll to his left (Figs. 68, 69).

Just as **B** is again about to recover his balance, **A** turns both pairs of wrists counterclockwise. This causes **B** to flip over again and roll to his right (Figs. 70–74).

75   76

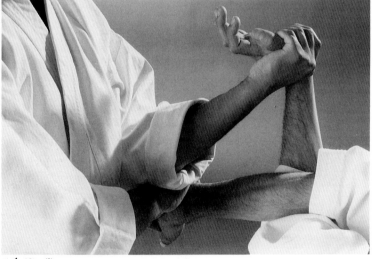

76¹ *(detail)*

Just as **B** is about to come out of his roll, **A** presses each of **B**'s arms against the other while maintaining control of the wrists, forming a crossed-arm tie (Figs. 75–76¹).

A raises his left leg, chambering it in order to give initial momentum to his next movement (Fig. 77).

A, turning both his and **B**'s left wrist clockwise, simultaneously moves them to his left, and steps down again to his left. This causes **B** to begin turning clockwise while he is still in a kneeling position (Figs. 78–79¹).

142   Zen Shaolin Karate

77

78   79

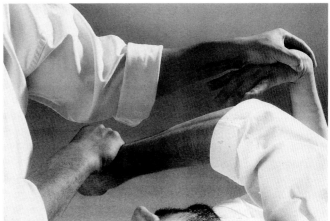

79¹ *(detail)*

80   81

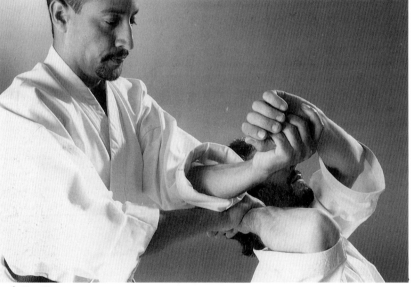

81[1] *(detail)*

A then raises his right leg and chambers it in order to maintain the momentum of his circular movement (Fig. 80).

A simultaneously moves both his and the opponent's wrists to his right, steps down again to his right, and then

82

82^1 (detail)

turns both his and B's left wrist counterclockwise. This causes B to continue turning on his knees, under A's arms, turning his back toward A (Figs. 81, 81^1).

A draws both his and B's hands to the right side of his body, causing B to continue turning, and completely lose his balance (Figs. 82, 82^1).

83

84

85

A moves both his and **B**'s hands to his left and then releases both of **B**'s hands. This causes **B** to continue turning until he is dumped on the ground (Figs. 83–85).

Once **B** has returned to a standing position, **A** continues by mirroring the previous movements (refer to pp. 136–146), after reassuming in the Nai Fuan Chin starting position.

146

86   87

88   89

Nai Fuan Chin Section Two
Solo Sequence

As with Section One, assume the raised crossed-hands posture and then the lowered crossed-hands posture (Figs. 86, 87).

Cross the wrists, turn the right palm to face upward, and step to the right with the left leg into a crossed-leg stance. Clench both hands into Nai Fuan Chin fists, and position them in front of and close to the chest, pointing toward each other with the palms facing downward (Figs. 88, 89).

90   91   92

Chamber the right leg, bending the knee forward and raising it. Increase the right elbow's angle to approximately 90 degrees, and move the elbow downward and inward. Turn the arm in a vertical arc about the elbow until the fist is in front of the right shoulder with the palm facing inward. Move the left fist under and touching the right elbow with the palm still facing downward, so that the forearm is almost horizontal and parallel to the chest (Figs. 90, 91).

Step to the right with the right leg into a straddle-leg stance. Keep the right elbow at a 90-degree angle while moving the fist outward and slightly backward. Simultaneously turn the right fist counterclockwise so that the back of the fist is facing the head (Fig. 92).

Step to the right with the left leg into a crossed-leg stance. Turn the right fist so that its back is facing forward once again and move the fist inward and slightly forward. Keep the right elbow at a 90-degree angle, and restore the elbow to its position above and touching the left fist (Fig. 93).

Step to the right with the right leg into the straddle-leg stance, and rotate the shoulders clockwise 45 degrees (Fig. 94).

148   Zen Shaolin Karate

93   94

95   96

Rotate the shoulders counterclockwise so that they are again facing directly forward. Open the right hand, and move it and the left fist to the right side of the body, so that the left fist is pointing toward and touching the right vertical palm (Fig. 95).

Swing the left fist up to shoulder height and across to a position slightly wide of the left shoulder with the palm turned inward. Keep the elbows down and maintain the left elbow's 90-degree angle. The right palm slides down to the lower left forearm as the left arm extends (Fig. 96).

97   98

99   100

Shift all the body weight to the right leg and chamber
the left leg by bending the knee forward and raising it. Pull
the hands to the left side of the body so the left fist is pointing forward with the palm facing upward. The right palm is

101

102

held with the fingers extended to the left and the palm facing the body (Fig. 97).

Step to the left with the left leg back into the straddle-leg stance. Keep the right elbow down while moving the open right hand and left arm upwards to chest height and across to the right so that the palm of the left fist is facing downward (Figs. 98, 99).

Open the left hand and move it outward in a horizontal counterclockwise arc finishing at chest height. Do not fully straighten the arm. Clench the right hand into a Nai Fuan Chin fist, and pull it to the right side of the body with the fingers pointing forward with the palm facing upward (Figs. 100, 101).

Clench the left hand into a Nai Fuan Chin fist, and pull it to the left side of the body with the palm facing upward. Move the right fist in front of the body with the palm facing downward so that the forearm is parallel to the chest but with the fist slightly lower than the elbow (Fig. 102).

103

104

Step to the left with the right leg into a crossed-leg stance, and then chamber the left leg by bending the knee forward and raising it (Figs. 103, 104).

Step to the left with your left leg into a straddle-leg stance. Keep the right elbow at a 90-degree angle and move it downward while positioning the right fist in front of the right shoulder with the palm facing inward (Figs. 105, 106).

Move the left fist forward and downward. Reposition both fists by moving the elbows slightly outward, then back inward, moving them in elbow-centered, counterclockwise semicircles. At the end of this movement, the right arm is fully straightened and the left fist positioned in front of the left shoulder (Figs. 107–109).

152   Zen Shaolin Karate

105

106

107

108

109

Chapter Four: Nai Fuan Chin

153

110

111

112

Keeping the upper arm in the same position, move the right fist under the left arm so it touches the left elbow, with the palm facing downward (Fig. 110).

Return to the lowered crossed-hands posture (Figs. 111, 112).

To complete Nai Fuan Chin Section Two, mirror the previous movements (refer to pp. 147–154), finishing in the lowered crossed-hands posture.

113

114

115

Nai Fuan Chin Section Two
Application

Start in the Nai Fuan Chin starting position (Fig. 113).

A does a cross step sideways to his right by moving his left leg across and in front of his right. He reverses both of B's grips by applying the combined underhand grip and overhand grip. A, his arms no longer crossed, establishes a firm grip on each of B's hands. A, turning his own and the opponent's right hand counterclockwise, raises both wrists in front of his chest (Figs. 114, 115).

116

117

118

119

120

121

156

121[1] *(another view)*

A raises his right leg, giving impetus to his next movement. A presses B's right arm against his left by turning both his and B's right wrist clockwise. This folds B's wrist, thereby forming a crossed-arm tie (Fig. 116).

A steps down and extends B's arms to his right, turning the right wrist counterclockwise and maintaining control of B's left wrist. This causes B to move to his left (Fig. 117).

A moves to the right with B using a cross step. He turns both his and B's right wrist clockwise and presses B's right arm, wrist folded again, back against B's left arm, reforming the crossed-arm tie. This causes B to begin to turn to his left (Figs. 118, 119).

A continues to move to the right, increasing the pressure of the crossed-arm tie. This causes B to turn clockwise as far as he can, until he is locked with his back toward and up against A's right side (Figs. 120–121[1]).

122¹ *(another view)*

122

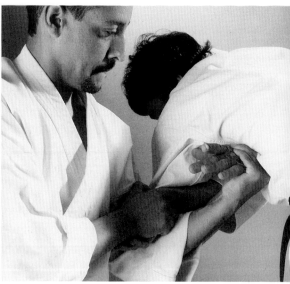

123¹ *(detail)*

123

Zen Shaolin Karate

124 125 126

B attempts to recover his balance by moving to his left and turning counterclockwise. A feels this and leads B in the direction of his intended movement. A folds B's left wrist and draws both wrists to the left side of B's body. Then, A folds B's left arm under and around B's right forearm, forming another crossed-arm tie and forcing B up onto his toes (Figs. 122–123[1]).

A simultaneously draws both wrists to the left side of his body and raises his left leg, unbalancing B and chambering the leg to give added impetus to his next movement (Fig. 124).

A steps down to his left again, and folding B's left arm above his right arm, moves both wrists to a position in front of B's chest, and then presses them down. This forces B down onto one knee (Figs. 125, 126).

Chapter Four: Nai Fuan Chin

127

128

129

130

131

Zen Shaolin Karate

132

133

134

A simultaneously extends both his and B's left arm to his left and draws the right wrists to the right side of his body. This causes B to roll to his right (Figs. 127–131).

A simultaneously draws his own and B's left wrist to the left side of his body and moves the right wrists to the front, maintaining the momentum of B's roll. Using a cross-step, A moves sideways with B in the direction of the roll, and keeps control of B's wrists. As B is about to come out of his roll, A raises his left leg, chambering it in order to give power to his next movement (Figs. 132–134).

135　　　　　　　　　　　　　　136

At the moment **B** is about to recover his balance, **A** steps down to his left and turns his and **B**'s right wrist clockwise. This causes **B** to flip over and roll in the opposite direction (Figs. 135, 136).

As **B** is again about to recover his balance, **A** turns both wrists counterclockwise. This causes **B** to flip over again and roll to his right (Figs. 137–139).

Just as **B** is about to come out of his roll, **A**, maintaining control of the wrists, presses each of **B**'s arms against the other, forming a crossed-arm tie (Figs. 140, 141).

Once **B** has regained his balance and returned to a standing position, **A** continues by mirroring the previous movements (refer to pp. 155–163), after reassuming the Nai Fuan Chin starting position.

　　　　　　　　　　Zen Shaolin Karate

137

138

139

140

141

142   143   144

Nai Fuan Chin Section Three
Solo Sequence

As with Sections One and Two, assume the raised crossed-hands posture and then the lowered crossed-hands posture (Figs. 142, 143).

Cross the wrists and turn both palms to face upward. Chamber the left leg by bending the knee forward and raising it while clenching each hand into a Nai Fuan Chin fist. Keep the elbows down and the wrists crossed, and position the fists in front of the chin with the palms facing inward (Fig. 144).

Step to the left with the left leg into a straddle-leg stance. Position the right fist in front of the right shoulder with the palm facing inward. The right elbow's angle is still 90 degrees. Position the left fist in front of the left thigh with the palm facing inward so the elbow is straight and at the same height as that of the other arm (Fig. 145).

Reposition both fists by moving the elbows slightly outward and back inward and moving the fists in elbow-

145

146

147

148

centered, counterclockwise semicircles. The right arm is fully straightened, with the palm inward, and the left fist positioned in front of the left shoulder with the palm inward (Figs. 146–148).

149

150

151

152

Mirror the previous repositioning of the fists by using clockwise instead of the counterclockwise movements (Figs. 149–151).

Keeping the upper arm in the same position, move the left fist so it touches the right elbow, with the palm facing downward (Fig. 152).

Zen Shaolin Karate

153

154

155

156

Open the left hand, and pull the right fist to the right side of the body with the fingers pointing forward and the palm facing upward. Move the fist forward so that the fully straightened arm is under and touching the left palm, and turn the fist over so its palm is facing downward (Figs. 153–156).

157   158   159

Move the right fist across to the left and backward. Then move it forward and outward with the palm facing upward, and step to the right with the left leg into a crossed-leg stance (Figs. 157–159). Step with the right leg to the right into a straddle-leg stance, and rotate the shoulders clockwise 45 degrees (Fig. 160).

Clench the left hand into a Nai Fuan Chin fist, and move both hands, in large counterclockwise circles, upward to the left. The right fist passes between the left arm and the chest, and the palm turns to face downward (Figs. 161, 162). Rotate the shoulders counterclockwise so they face directly forward again (Fig. 163). Extend the arms across the chest (Fig. 164). Open the left hand and move the right fist in a horizontal counterclockwise arc to the right side of the body.

168

160   161   162

163   164

165

166

167

168

169

170　　　　　　　　171　　　　　　　172

The left palm faces downward and the right palm faces upward (Fig. 165). Move the right fist forward until it is fully straightened. Turn the fist over so the palm is facing downward (Figs. 166, 167).

Move the open left hand outward, with the palm facing forward, in a counterclockwise arc finishing at chest height. Do not fully straighten the arm. Pull the right fist to the right side of the body with the fingers pointing forward and the palm facing upward (Figs. 168, 169).

Clench the left hand into a Nai Fuan Chin fist, and pull it to the left side of the body with the palm facing upward. Move the right fist in front of the body with the palm facing downward (Fig. 170). The right forearm is parallel to the chest with the fist slightly lower than the elbow. Step to the left with the right foot into a crossed-leg stance, and then chamber the left leg by bending the knee forward and raising it (Figs. 171, 172).

173

174

175

176

177

172

Zen Shaolin Karate

178 179 180

Step to the left with the left leg into a straddle-leg stance (Fig. 173). Turn the right arm in a vertical arc about the elbow so that the fist is positioned in front of the right shoulder, with the palm facing inward (Fig. 174).

Move the left fist forward and downward. Move the elbows slightly outward and back inward, and move the fists in elbow-centered, counterclockwise semicircles. The right arm is fully straightened and the left fist is positioned in front of the left shoulder (Figs. 175–177).

Keeping the left upper arm in the same position, move the right fist under the left arm so it touches the left elbow, with the palm facing downward (Fig. 178).

Return to the lowered crossed-hands posture (Figs. 179, 180).

181

182

To complete Nai Fuan Chin Section Three, mirror the previous movements (refer to pp. 164–173), finishing in the lowered crossed-hands posture.

Finish by performing the *gassho* and return to the attention posture (Figs. 181, 182).

174

183

184

Nai Fuan Chin Section Three Application

Start in the Nai Fuan Chin starting position (Fig. 183).

A reverses both of B's grips by applying the double underhand grip. A raises his left leg, adding impetus to his next arm movement. He folds both of B's wrists, and raises them in front of his chin (Fig. 184).

185

186

187

188

A steps down to his left and after uncrossing his arms, extends both his and B's left arm downward. He turns both his own and B's left wrist clockwise and presses each of B's arms against the other, forming a crossed-arm tie. B is then forced down onto one knee (Figs. 185, 186).

As B is about to recover his posture, A, pressing B's forearms against one another, rotates the wrists in a coun-

176   Zen Shaolin Karate

189

190

191

192

terclockwise direction. This causes **B** to roll to his right (Figs. 187, 188).

Just as **B** is again about to regain his balance, **A**, pressing **B**'s forearms against one another, rotates the wrists in a clockwise direction. This causes **B** to roll to his left (Figs. 189–192).

193

194

A allows **B**'s wrists to rotate within his hands, changing to a double overhand grip. Just as **B** is about to come out of his roll, **A** presses **B**'s arms against one another, forming a crossed-arm tie (Figs. 193, 194).

178

195

196

197

As **B** attempts to recover his balance, **A** draws both his own and **B**'s right wrist to his right side. **A** then pushes the right wrist forward and turns it counterclockwise. This causes **B** to roll to his right (Figs. 195–197).

198

199

200

201

202

203

Zen Shaolin Karate

204

205

Just as **B** is about to recover his balance, **A**, pressing **B**'s forearms against one another, rotates the right wrist around the left in a clockwise manner. This causes **B** to turn under the arms and roll clockwise to his left (Figs. 198–203).

A keeps **B**'s forearms pressed against each other and moves sideways in the direction of the turn or roll. He keeps **B** off balance by moving both wrists in this same direction (Figs. 204, 205).

206

207

208

209

Again, as **B** is about to recover his balance, **A**, keeping each of **B**'s forearms pressed against the other, rotates his right wrist around the left one in a counterclockwise direction. This causes **B** to turn under the arms and roll counterclockwise to his right (Figs. 206–209).

Zen Shaolin Karate

Once more, as **B** is about to recover his balance, **A** draws the right wrist to his right side. He then pushes it forward, beneath the left wrist, and turns both wrists counterclockwise. This causes **B** to roll clockwise to his left (Figs. 210–213).

214

215

A, in one movement, extends B's left arm to his left and draws his own and B's right wrist to the right side of his body. This causes B to begin to roll to his right (Figs. 214, 215).

A simultaneously draws his own and B's left wrist to the left side of his body and moves B's right wrist in front of his body, maintaining the momentum of B's roll. A moves sideways with B, in the direction of the roll, and keeps control of B's arms. As B is about to come out of his roll, A raises his left leg, chambering it in order to give power to his next movement (Figs. 216–218).

Just as B is about to regain his balance, A steps down to his left and turns B's right wrist clockwise. This causes B to flip over and roll to his left (Figs. 219, 220).

216

217

218

219

220

221   222   223

224   225

At the moment that **B** is again about to recover his balance, **A** turns both wrists counterclockwise. This causes **B** to flip over yet again and roll to his right (Figs. 221–225).

Just as **B** is about to come out of his roll, **A**, maintain-

226

227

ing control of the wrists, presses each of **B**'s arms against the other, forming a crossed-arm tie (Figs. 226, 227).

Once **A** allows **B** to regain his balance and return to a standing position, **A** continues by mirroring the previous movements (refer to pp. 175–187), after reassuming the Nai Fuan Chin starting position.

Chapter Five

Pushing Hands

Kung fu has received nearly all the limelight as far as softness, flowing movement, and pushing hands are concerned. Indeed, many karate-ka have studied t'ai-chi ch'uan and other 'soft' arts to find something that exists within their own art. Although partially retained by Naha stylists, such as Goju-ryu practitioners, pushing hands is the heritage of all who have inherited the techniques and principles once developed at the Shaolin Temple.

What is pushing hands? How can it be practiced? In the beginning, pushing hands requires three elements: a partner, contact, and flowing force. Practitioners position themselves so that their forearms are connected in the various positional combinations that characterize this practice. They then both begin to apply a forward pressure. This pressure is called 'weaving silk' by the Chinese and it is maintained as the practitioners rhythmically flow from movement to movement trying not to lose the flow or 'break the thread' of contact. The forearms are thus trained to become sensitive to force. This does not mean that the arms become delicate, but rather that they acquire abilities similar to those of insects' antennae, efficiently sensing danger.

Put simply, pushing hands skills are the skills of defense by touch. This might not sound much like karate to some until it is realized that pushing hands is much more than a separate auxiliary exercise. Many of the more profound principles and techniques contained in kata can best be expressed and demonstrated through pushing hands. An examination of the many movements in karate kata shows that they are not all defenses against the charging straight punches and high kicks frequently found in modern karate.

Pushing hands drills allow a greater variety of contact practice, including grappling-type movements. Many karate-ka feel uncomfortable during close-quarter combat and pushing hands is the perfect vehicle for overcoming this discomfort.

Theories and Concepts

The pushing hands practice of Zen Shaolin karate is the method used to link kata with spontaneous application. Its purpose, as previously stated, is to develop and maintain a practitioner's ability to detect, redirect, and counter all types of force by contact reflex. The basic drills are practiced in a fixed position and train the body to deflect simple pushing forces either by turning at the waist or by transferring the force from one hand to the other. This makes it possible to deal effectively with superior force. The theory can be encapsulated in the following rhyme:

> Yield to a force
> and bend its angle,
> this will avoid
> an ugly tangle.

After basic fixed pushing hands practice, one may progress to moving pushing hands, Saam Chin boxing, and Nai Fuan Chin grappling. For those interested in applying techniques from traditional kata, the emphasis on the contact range during pushing hands practice will reveal the importance of this traditional method of sparring. It is only at this contact distance that all hands-on techniques in the kata can be made to work in combinations, and most importantly, without prearrangement. Pushing hands will enable you to sharpen your reflexes, borrow an opponent's force, and cover, trap, and neutralize all manner of attacks. Finally, it will contribute tremendously to the technical repertoire of anyone who practices it.

Practicing Pushing Hands

In the following section, you will be introduced to the basic drills of pushing hands and how to use them as a medium to apply the techniques in the Saam Chin and Nai Fuan Chin kata. Practice the following exercises slowly and smoothly. Try to keep the pressure constant but without straining. Above all else, be attentive to how your opponent telegraphs his intentions through subtle movements you can feel in your arms rather than those that you can see.

1

The Fixed Pushing Hands Drill

Fixed pushing hands is conducted by assuming the pushing hands starting position shown (Fig. 1). Each person is in the Saam Chin stance and is standing on the circumference of a personal circle. Contact is established where these two circles meet.

A degree of partner cooperation is required in the early stages of learning and practicing. Combat is not implied and competition (*i.e.*, trying to 'get one in') will be detrimental to progress. A well-established and effective method of attaining cooperation is for each individual to put the needs of the other first. Using this method, and by providing the correct amount of force, you can help your partner produce the appropriate response. The easiest way to establish a good pushing hands repertoire is to assign the roles of attacker and defender. One person will be the driver, the initiator of the action, and the other will be a passenger along for the ride, responding to the other's actions.

This basic pushing hands method is used to get the feel of a training partner. These movements can be related to the movements of Section Two of the Saam Chin kata. Try to ensure that you turn at the waist to deflect the force. Also, it is important to make sure that when you push, you do so toward the center of your partner's body.

2   3

4   5

From the pushing hands starting position, **B** pushes toward **A**'s center. **A** turns at the waist, neutralizing the push (Figs. 2, 3). **A** begins to return the push (Fig. 4). **B** turns at the waist, neutralizing the push (Fig. 5). **B** begins to return the push (Fig. 6). **A** turns at the waist, neutralizing the push (Fig. 7). Continue going back and forth smoothly pushing and deflecting.

6

7

8

9

10

Changing Sides

Once you have built up confidence in the fixed pushing hands drill, you can change sides using the Saam Chin circle step. From the last position in the fixed pushing hands drill, retreat by sweeping your left leg in and back (Figs. 8–10). Try to keep the body at the same height as you step, and do not let the contact arm collapse. You can then begin to push hands on the other side.

11

12

Basic Changes

This set of basic drills encourages sensitivity to an opponent's force and helps reduce the urge to blindly resist an attack as the body learns to adapt to and flow with whatever comes. At first, these changes should be learned and practiced lightly, without moving from the Saam Chin stance. When you can move the arms independently of each other and the body, and neutralize basic attacks by turning at the waist, you will be ready to coordinate these changes with moving steps. These should be learned and practiced on both sides.

194   Zen Shaolin Karate

13

14

15

Change One: From the pushing hands starting position, **A** begins to return **B**'s push (Fig. 11). **B** turns at the waist, neutralizing the push. This time, **B** does not push back toward the center, but pushes across his midline toward **A**'s right side (Fig. 12). Instead of turning at the waist, **A** transfers the force over to his right hand (Figs. 13, 14). **A** begins to return the push using his right hand (Fig. 15).

16

17

18

Zen Shaolin Karate

19

20

B diverts A's push by pushing it across the center toward A's left side (Fig. 16). A crosses underneath and transfers the force over to his left hand (Fig. 17). A pushes back in toward the center (Fig. 18). A and B resume fixed pushing hands (Figs. 19, 20).

21

22

Change Two: From the pushing hands starting position, **A** pushes at **B** (Fig. 21). **B** diverts **A**'s push by pressing into his left arm and trapping it (Fig. 22). This puts **A** in a poor position and, in Saam Chin boxing, **B** might well follow this arm trap with a left back-fist strike. **A** crosses underneath and transfers the force to his right hand (Figs. 23, 24). **B** also crosses underneath and transfers the force to his left hand. He has now gained an inside position and is ready to push back (Fig. 25).

23

24

25

26

27

28

As **B** pushes back with his left hand, **A** transfers the force to his left hand (Figs. 26, 27). **A** and **B** then resume fixed pushing hands (Figs. 28, 29).

Zen Shaolin Karate

29

30

31

Change Three: From the pushing hands starting position, A pushes at B (Fig. 30). B threads his right hand under and pushes A's supporting right hand across the midline (Fig. 31). A crosses underneath and transfers the force to his left

32

33

34

35

hand, gaining an inside position, and begins to push back
(Figs. 32, 33). **B** crosses underneath and transfers the force
to his left hand (Figs. 34, 35). **A** and **B** resume fixed pushing hands (Fig. 36).

Zen Shaolin Karate

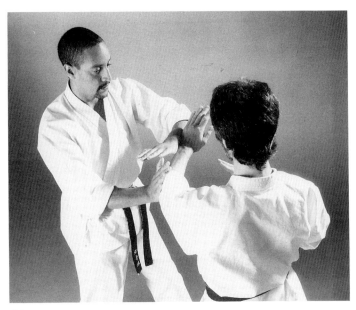

36

Introducing Saam Chin Boxing into Pushing Hands Practice

The basic pushing hands changes demonstrated thus far were derived from movements in Sections One and Two of the Saam Chin kata. This section will concentrate on the application of movements from Section Three in pushing hands practice, in particular, how to defend against basic strikes and kicks. You will find the method easier to apply if you consistently use the rear hand as the significator.

This photo sequence will take you through a systematic set of responses to basic attacks. Work slowly and smoothly through them. By experimenting with slow punches and kicks, you will be able to feel the forces and their directions, and will be able to redirect them. All sensible pushing hands changes were discovered this way and you can learn them for yourself.

37

38

39

40

Defense Against a Lead-hand Back-fist Strike: From the
pushing hands starting position, instead of pushing, **B** aims
a left back-fist strike at **A** (Fig. 37). **A** intercepts and guides
it away from his body using the ulnar side of the forearm

41

42

43

(Fig. 38). He then traps it and counters with a palm-heel strike (Figs. 39, 40). As **B** retracts his extended left hand, **A** pushes into the center with his left hand. **A** and **B** resume fixed pushing hands (Figs. 41–43).

44
        45

·46
        47

Defense Against an Upper-level Rear-hand Straight Punch: From the pushing hands starting position, instead of pushing, **B** aims a straight right punch at **A**'s face (Fig. 44). **A** intercepts and leads it away from his body using the ulnar side of the forearm (Fig. 45). He then traps it and counters

48

49

50

51

with a right palm-heel strike (Figs. 46, 47). As **B** retracts
his extended right hand, **A** pushes into the center (Figs. 48,
49). **B** transfers the force over to his left hand (Fig. 50). **A**
and **B** resume fixed pushing hands (Fig. 51).

52

53

54

Defense Against a Rear-hand Back-fist Strike: From the pushing hands starting position, instead of pushing, **B** aims a right back-fist strike at **A** (Fig. 52). **A** intercepts and leads it away from his body using the radial side of the forearm

208   Zen Shaolin Karate

55

56

57

58

(Fig. 53). He then traps **B**'s attacking arm and counters with a right palm heel (Figs. 54–56). As **B** retracts his extended right hand, **A** pushes into the center (Figs. 57, 58).

59

60   61

B transfers the force to his left hand (Fig. 59). A and
B resume fixed pushing hands (Figs. 60, 61).

**Defense Against an Upper-level Lead-hand Straight
Punch from a Crossed Position:** From the pushing hands

210

62

63

64

65

starting position, instead of pushing, **B** threads his right hand
through and opens up **A**'s corner (Figs. 62, 63). **A** immediately transfers the force to his left hand (Fig. 64). **B** aims a
straight left punch at **A** (Fig. 65).

66

67

68

A intercepts and guides it away using the radial side of the forearm (Fig. 66). He then traps **B**'s arm and counters with a right palm-heel strike (Figs. 67, 68). As **B** retracts his extended left hand, **A** pushes back into the center (Figs. 69, 70). **A** and **B** resume fixed pushing hands (Fig. 71).

212

69

70

71

72

73

Defense Against a Middle-level Hook Punch from a Crossed Position: From the pushing hands starting position, instead of pushing, B threads his right hand through and opens up A's corner (Figs. 72, 73). A immediately transfers the force over to his left hand (Fig. 74). B aims a left hook punch at the body of A, who intercepts it by dropping

214

74

75

76

77

his right hand, the significator, to his right front corner, and
transfers the force to his left hand (Figs. 75, 76). A slips his
left arm underneath **B**'s forward arm and strikes **B**'s body
with a left palm-heel strike (Fig. 77). **A**'s fingers are facing
down when he performs this strike.

78

79

80

81

    B drops his left hand and sticks to **A**'s left hand (Figs.
78, 79). **A** and **B** resume fixed pushing hands (Figs. 80, 81).

216

84

Defense Against a Foot Sweep: As A pushes, B moves to A's side into the crossed-leg stance, and then tries to sweep his left leg (Figs. 82–84).

A, responding to the touch pressure (not to knowledge of the sequence) raises his left leg and converts the force to a low side kick aimed at **B**'s supporting leg (Figs. 85–87). **A** retracts his kicking leg and both he and **B** step down and resume fixed pushing hands (Figs. 88–90).

88

89

90

Chapter Five: Pushing Hands

91

92

93

Defense Against a Front Kick, Lead-hand Straight Punch Combination: B pushes A out of contact range and attacks with a middle-level front kick (Figs. 91–93). A momentarily contacts B's attacking leg with his right hand, his significator, before transferring the force to his left hand, which passes over the top (Figs. 94, 95). B places his kicking leg down, and aims a straight left punch at A (Fig. 96).

220   Zen Shaolin Karate

94

95

96

97

98

99

100

A intercepts and deflects it with the radial side of his left forearm (Fig. 97). He then traps B's arm and counters with a right palm-heel strike (Fig. 98). As B retracts his extended left hand, A pushes back into the center, and they resume fixed pushing hands (Figs. 99, 100).

222   Zen Shaolin Karate

101

102

Introducing Nai Fuan Chin Grappling into Pushing Hands

Because pushing hands is a contact medium, practice sessions that include grappling need not be conducted in stop-start fashion. By using pushing hands, you will be able to maintain contact while smoothly mixing and matching boxing with grappling. You will thus be able to practice in a continuous and free-flowing style.

Set One: From the pushing hands starting position, **B** pushes toward A's center. A turns at the waist, neutralizing the push (Figs. 101, 102).

103

104

105

A then traps **B**'s left arm, and presses against the elbow, bringing him to his knees (Figs. 103–105). As he shifts
into a Nai Fuan Chin stance, he grabs **B**'s left hand and turns
it, locking the wrist. He then rotates **B**'s arm back, locking
his shoulder (Fig. 106). The pressure of this hold forces **B**

224   Zen Shaolin Karate

106

107

108

109

to roll backward (Fig. 107). **A** releases the hold on **B**'s hand, allowing him to come back up (Fig. 108). As **A** shifts back into the Saam Chin stance, **B** returns to a standing position and they resume fixed pushing hands (Fig. 109).

110   111

112

Set Two: From the pushing hands starting position, **B** pushes toward A's center. A turns at the waist, neutralizing the push (Figs. 110, 111). A then traps B's left arm and shifts into a cat stance (Fig. 112). A shifts into a Nai Fuan Chin

Zen Shaolin Karate

113

114

115

stance while applying a wrist lock, adding momentum to his throw (Fig. 113). **A** continues to turn **B**'s wrist, making him roll over (Figs. 114, 115).

116

117

118

119

A turns B's hand the other way and uses his right hand to make B roll in the opposite direction (Figs. 116, 117). As A shifts back into the Saam Chin stance, he allows B to return to a standing position so they can resume fixed pushing hands (Figs. 118, 119).

Zen Shaolin Karate

120

121

122

123

Set Three: From the pushing hands starting position, instead of pushing, **B** aims a straight right punch at **A**'s face. **A** intercepts and leads it away from his body with the ulnar side of his right forearm (Figs. 120, 121). He transfers the force over to his left hand and grabs **B**'s wrist (Figs. 122, 123).

124

125

126

127

He then turns the hand as he raises it and shifts into the Nai Fuan Chin stance, putting pressure on B's wrist joint, bringing B to his knees (Figs. 124, 125). A pushes on the back of B's neck as he cranks the locked arm over, forcing B to roll (Figs. 126–129). A turns B's hand the other

130

131

way, forcing him to roll in the opposite direction. As A shifts back into the Saam Chin stance, he allows **B** to return to a standing position and they can then resume fixed pushing hands (Figs. 130, 131).

Chapter Six

Final Thoughts

As we have seen, Zen Shaolin karate is more than a mere style of karate. It is a set of theories and principles that can be applied by any martial artist, be he a karate-ka or a practitioner of a different system. In this chapter, I will summarize how these theories are applied through a brief list of maxims, and before concluding, will include a parable that encapsulates a number of the teachings of Zen Shaolin karate.

Some Maxims

To begin, the following are a series of brief but important proverbs that you should keep in mind as you are training:

- Once the kicking distance is closed, keep it closed.
- Combinations occur in response to an opponent's actions, not because they are your favorite set of techniques.
- Control and strike the opponent at the same instant.
- Openings are felt with contact, not seen with the eye.
- Seek control of an opponent's posture as a prerequisite to a counterattack.
- Always deflect, parry, cover, and trap. These defenses are superior to direct blocks.
- Footwork and position are a major part of the battle in unbalancing and controlling an opponent who is committed to attack.
- Dodging, ducking, and weaving require a high degree of physical stamina and are unnecessary if the opponent's attacking limbs are being properly controlled.

- Everything moves from the *hara*.
- In defense, be like the dragonfly that perches on the stick raised to hit it.
- Full mastery of one technique is better than the incomplete mastery of two.

Chu and the Watermelon

There was much hustle and bustle. Soldiers were swaggering around with the kind of walk that takes up more space than is necessary. In the marketplace, business was brisk. There were peddlers, money-changers, and all manner of street vendors, all noisily plying their trades.

Chu looked for the clearing, and soon found it. Street entertainers and colorful actors crowded around, speaking in strange dialects. He could hear the faint but constant drone of chanting monks as he edged his way through the crowd. Some people made way for him while others ignored the young man, dressed in the robes of a novice Buddhist monk. Chu raised his hand, in greeting and salutation, to an itinerant monk who joined him in the crowd. They both looked into the clearing.

Thwack! Tung Chih hit the watermelon so hard that it split into two pieces in midair, scattering melon pips into the crowd, which cheered and applauded. Tung Chih, a fighting man, was dressed in the standard Manchu costume, consisting of a loose side-fastening jacket worn over a tunic and pants. The red jacket of this Manchu bannerman was emblazoned with a dragon crest, which showed him to be a member of the first of eight military companies of the new dynasty. This man, who was so unlike Chu's teacher, Master Tao Sheng, impressed the novice. He doubted whether Tao Sheng could display the sheer, vibrant power that Tung Chih had used to split the melon.

The Manchu bannerman left the enclosure amidst cheers and hearty congratulations on his fine spear-hand strike. He was replaced by a beggar monk who wasted no time in assuming a curious, birdlike posture over a table upon which rested a fresh watermelon. With a strange cry, the monk thrust down at the melon and pierced it with a three-finger strike. Seizing the melon and gripping it with the striking hand, the monk succeeded in breaking off a small piece. This time the crowd was not so impressed and the monk, having been politely applauded, left the enclosure to be replaced by an announcer, who declared Tung Chih to be the winner.

Chu was sorry that he constantly broke monastic rules, but it was all so difficult and he was one of the lucky ones. His commitment to the order was of his own choice; it wasn't a case of filial piety or family poverty. Still he sometimes wondered whether he had made the right decision. He recalled vividly the sheer destructive power of Tung Chih's spear-hand strike, and the bearing of the man: tall, strong, and proud. He remembered the cheering, and wished that it had been for him. Chu tried to recall Tao Sheng's teachings on the evil of pride, but his emotions made the teaching seem very boring. Here, in the marketplace, the world seemed different, very different indeed. He decided to go and see his teacher.

Passing the monastery kitchen, Chu spotted a large firm watermelon. In a moment of confused passion and emotion, his head filled with images of Tung Chih and lacking any real plan, he grabbed the melon and fled the kitchen. As luck would have it, he ran headlong into the venerable Tao Sheng. When asked for an explanation of his conduct, Chu blurted out his experiences at the marketplace, and proclaimed that he was thinking of leaving the monastery. After a pause, he concluded by challenging Tao Sheng to split the watermelon or at least teach him how to do it. Putting his head to one side and uttering 'tsks,' Tao Sheng addressed

Zen Shaolin Karate

Chu slowly and quietly, "I am surprised that our young men are so badly treated as to crave so for a slice of melon, and that our kitchen lacks the appropriate utensil to divide it." Taking the melon, Tao Sheng departed.

Dusk had long fallen and the temple was quiet. Chu was irritated by the crunch of dry leaves beneath his feet. The night air was cold and he felt as though he had waited an eternity for the old man to go to sleep. Peering cautiously into the old monk's room, he saw the melon was still there on the table, exactly where it had been all evening. Adrenaline ran through his body as he began to move closer to the prize. Chu quickly shrank back in hiding as Tao Sheng went into the chamber, picked up the melon and the table, and stepped outside. There he was joined by his old mentor and friend, Master Li Tsun Ya, who seemed to appear from nowhere.

Chu had heard many stories about Li Tsun Ya, but had never seen him practice. It was rumored that he practiced the Saam Chin form many times a day, and that his pushing hands practice was superb. Chu wondered how this could be, as Li Tsun Ya looked so frail and weak. True, he always appeared spirited, yet Chu had doubts. Chu's mind went back to the marketplace and the bannerman. Again he saw the melon pips scatter into the crowd. He remembered the smells, the faces, the voices, and the applause. He wanted to believe in his teachers, but he had doubts.

Li Tsun Ya moved briskly to the table, and standing close, assumed the Saam Chin stance at a slight angle to the table. The monk made sweeping, circular passes across his body with both arms, before requesting Tao Sheng to strike him. Tao Sheng aimed a powerful rear-hand straight punch at the head of the senior monk, who merely intercepted it with a circular parry. Chu watched as Master Li Tsun Ya deflected the force of the blow to the other side of his body, and redirected it toward the melon. The seemingly weak and ineffectual palm-heel strike caused the melon to roll off the table and onto the ground with a harmless plop, whereupon both monks retired inside.

Chu could barely control himself or his bitter disappointment. He resolved to salvage the melon and at least put on a better performance than the charade he had just witnessed. Creeping close, he reached for the discarded melon and tried to pick it up. It was floppy and misshapen and the inside was a complete liquid mush, yet the skin was unbroken! Then it dawned upon Chu: they had known that he was watching them.

The next day, the morning dharma lecture was given by Tao Sheng, who took the high seat in the Eighteen Lohan Hall. He said, "If a way to the truth is pointed out, and you feel it through practice, you will know it utterly and with your whole being. The experience will be your own. I can demonstrate my understanding a hundred times, but that will never make it your understanding. *Ch'an* is not a belief system, so it is no good merely believing what I say. You must investigate the truth for yourself during practice. The path is not traveled by being impressed with others. All that can do is entertain you, or produce a temporary bubble of inspiration that will burst when pricked by the sharp needle of reality. The true key is to be found in practice, practice, and more practice, and by paying attention to the truth, not the appearance. Both practical and fringe empty-hand skills are like the *siddhis* or mystical powers of yoga. They are side benefits, not goals. If you chase them, they will lead you off the path."

Rearranging his robes and stepping down from the high seat, Tao Sheng departed. The other monks began to file out of the hall for morning practice of the forms. Only Chu remained to ponder the teaching of the watermelon.

Zen Shaolin Karate

Conclusion

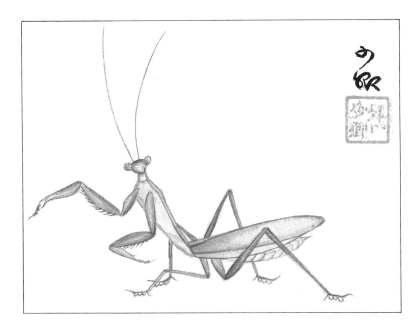

The discovery of the Nai Fuan Chin and Saam Chin applications demanded that this book be written. The fact that the proper applications had disappeared provided considerable food for thought, as well as posing something of a dilemma. If, before the creation of the Pinan forms, the Nai Fuan Chin kata were the basis of the karate taught by the prominent nineteenth-century teacher Anko Itosu, then why were the applications missing?

Three possibilities suggest themselves. The first possibility is that the true teachings were kept secret and only one or two worthy students were allowed to learn a particular teacher's entire system. The second possibility, and one that is presently popular, is that kata have multiple levels of *bunkai* (applications), the highest of which are too dangerous to be taught to any but the most trusted student(s). The third possibility is that some early founders of Okinawan karate may not have known the functions of certain kata.

Dealing with the third possibility first, during the spring of 1992, I met and spoke with one of Gichin Funakoshi's students, who told me that Funakoshi had taught no applications for the Nai Fuan Chin kata. Written instructions regarding the applications appeared in Funakoshi's book, *Karate-do Kyohan,* but they do not pertain to grappling and there are no illustrations. Another book by Funakoshi, *Karate-do Nyumon,* contains an account of the rigorous Tekki (Nai Fuan Chin) training that Funakoshi experienced under the guidance of Itosu, who was said to specialize in these kata. Funakoshi himself claimed to have walked eight kilometers daily to and from Itosu's house for ten years, during which time he studied only the Naihanchi (Nai Fuan Chin) kata. I have absolutely no doubt about the accuracy of Funakoshi's claims or the correctness of his character, intentions, or commitment to provide karate with a good, solid, ethical base. However, anecdotes, myths, and legends are only useful if they guide and inspire, without obscuring reality. During the period when Funakoshi was learning karate, there was a cultural pattern in which a student was not permitted to ask questions. If that approach was coupled with the belief (fostered by the absence of explanation) that endless solo repetitions of a given kata will ultimately reveal its purpose, then early karate teachers may not have known the applications of certain kata. Perhaps the earliest Okinawan students learned Nai Fuan Chin by observing a Chinese exponent practicing alone.

With regard to the claim that kata have multiple applications, I shall confine my view to the Nai Fuan Chin kata, which are clearly sequential. I reassert that function dictated form, and that things take on a shape or form according to their intended purpose or function. The function of the Nai Fuan Chin kata is clear and unambiguous, as all but the most recalcitrant of experienced karate-ka will be able to see.

Concerning the so-called dangerous applications, as we have seen (and despite the undoubted practicality of them), there is nothing in the Nai Fuan Chin applications that is any more dangerous than techniques from other empty-hand disciplines, such as jujutsu or aikido, which the Nai Fuan Chin kata predates. Of course, brutal personal ways of practicing the applications could be developed, but such a would-be expert would soon run out of training partners.

Finally, regarding the legends of secret traditions, it is difficult to believe that a teacher who cherishes a system would deny the benefit of it to the next generation. I concur that it might initially be necessary to withhold some practical skills from those whose character traits do not include the responsibility that must accompany such skills. The practice may not be suitable for all. However, the teacher's duty lies in the preservation and dissemination of his or her chosen way.

I have decided to let the kata speak for themselves as much as possible, as these kata, accurately passed on by some, tell a tale about the nobility of karate. Karate practice should ultimately aim at quelling the internal faults of the practitioner. This can be achieved by not clinging to subconscious fears or images of the bogeyman. Indeed, we need to divest such images of the crippling power they can have over our psyches. Thus, it is necessary to master the self before trying to master others! This is true victory.

How many people are going to practice karate year after year, just in case of the odd punch-up? In a practical way, karate teaches us how to keep out of or minimize trouble. This goal is achieved not by turning us into muscle-bound supermen, nor by making us excessively scholarly, nor polite in an insincere way. It is through hard training that we begin to understand the ego-centered, sometimes confused, sometimes selfish, small mind within ourselves and others. This develops genuine compassion, which is not to be confused with feeling sorry for other people. The truly skillful karate-ka then becomes uplifted, more powerful, and wiser in situations of potential or actual conflict. Although the foundation is the practical, physical skill itself, it is only a means to an end, and not the end in itself!

It is, of course, necessary to consider and face conflict in everyday life. Karate developed away from the root philosophy of Zen, however, often has the effect of pandering to an endless stream of subconscious images and scenarios, devised by a mind limited and stricken by its own fear.

For the final evidence of the nobility of karate, I turn once again to the ancient kata whose techniques, although practical, are subtle, complex, and require a high degree of control and skill to be applied. Can we seriously believe that no one in ancient China or Japan ever thought of using a head butt? Yet, to my knowledge, none of the ancient kata contain such a movement. Thus I conclude that the methodology behind the kata is fundamentally different from the pugilistic methods presented so often today.

What started out as a book about the Nai Fuan Chin and Saam Chin kata, has become a book about the whole of karate as my colleagues and I understand it. We hope that you will find it useful on your personal quest.

Conclusion